I invite you to come along on an unusual journey with Anna and Nate. I had a front row seat into the lives of two ordinary people who grew even closer through an unexpected twist. As you share in their story you will be reminded that we do not control our destiny. Our lives are in the hands of an amazing God. He decides when to give and when to take away. Our goal in this life is to bless His name regardless. Get ready for minute-by-minute details of bouncing back and forth between trust and anxiety. Let their story encourage you to go deeper in Christ.

DAN SEABORN,
President and Founder, Winning at Home Inc. Author, *Parenting with Grace and Truth*

Trusting in God with all of our hearts is not an easy thing to do. Human nature desires to be in control. Nate and Anna chose to rely on God, not just when things were going well, but when life itself seemed to be stripped from their hands. Because God remained at the center in their most difficult moments, His glory now shines brightly through their story. May it inspire you to trust God more fully in the days and years to come.

KIRK AND JULIE COUSINS,
Washington Redskins quarterback and wife

In his poem *"On Another's Sorrow,"* William Blake asked if the God Who "hears the wren with sorrows small, hears the small bird's grief and care" will not "sit beside the nest pouring pity in their breast?" In this little testament Anna and Nate Weeber share how that very God came early one morning to sit beside them in their bedroom, an ambulance, the hospital, the ICU, and then stayed for 18 grace-filled nights and days.

The Weebers wrote these words to honor God and to strengthen our faith. They succeed at both by sharing a mix of personal recounting and Facebook postings. Some lessons given us: the importance of faith ahead of time; the unbelievable support from the church community; the privilege of excellent medical care. Blake concludes, "Think not thou canst weep a tear and thy Maker is not near." The Weebers help us grow in grace.

REN BROEKHUIZEN,
Founding Pastor, Ridge Point Community Church, Holland, Michigan

18DAYS
OF
GRACE

18DAYS OF GRACE

A STORY OF GOD'S MIRACULOUS HEALING POWER

NATE & ANNA WEEBER

credo
house publishers

18 Days of Grace

Copyright © 2017 Nate and Anna Weeber

Published in the United States by Credo House Publishers,
a division of Credo Communications, LLC, Grand Rapids, Michigan
www.credohousepublishers.com

*All of the Facebook status updates in this book are the original posts
by Nate Weeber at the time of the aneurysm.*

All Scripture, unless otherwise indicated, are taken from the Holy Bible,
New International Version®, NIV®. Copyright © 1973, 1978, 1984, 2011 by Biblica, Inc.
Used by permission.

ISBN: 978-1-625860-80-4

Cover and interior design by Sharon VanLoozenoord
Editing by Donna Huisjen

Printed in the United States of America

First edition

DEDICATION

This book is dedicated to . . .

God. Father, we dedicate this book to You.
We are where we are today because of You.
We praise You for Your miraculous wonders.
May Your glory shine bright through this book!

Declan and Hudson, our two precious boys.
You bring so much life and joy to our lives.
We praise God for you and will love you forever!

Our thousands of prayer warriors.
You prayed in faith, expectantly, daily.
We will be forever grateful.

PROLOGUE

*"The will of God will never take you
where the Grace of God will not protect you."*

BERNADETTE DEVLIN

— ANNA'S STORY —

Something was wrong. It had to be. My head was pounding. It felt like there was a balloon in my head filling with tar—immediately full, but still trying to expand, like it had no more room to grow. The pressure was unlike anything I've experienced before. I sat on the edge of our bed, holding my head, praying God would take away just some of the pain. The room started spinning; I was sweating— it felt like it was 90 degrees in our house.

I've had many headaches before and even migraines while I've been pregnant in the past, but this . . . this was different. This came on so fast. Usually they intensify slowly, and I can tell when they're going to be bad. But this time it came on in the blink of an eye and its pain was unbearable from the start. It was then that I felt it. A nudge from the Holy Spirit to tell my husband, Nate, how serious this was.

Because I was twenty-six weeks pregnant, everything in me tried to convince me that this was just another routine pregnancy migraine. No big deal. I'd take some Tylenol and it'd be gone. No need to worry Nate. I normally try to downplay my discomforts when I'm not feeling well or have another headache. No need to make a big deal about nothing, right? Sometimes I feel like a dripping faucet when I tell Nate I have yet again, another headache. They happen so often—he doesn't need to be burdened with one more thing. But this nudge kept coming again and again. Each time I would push it away it would come back twice as strong.

Was this just in my head or was this for real? Did God really want me to tell my husband about this? He was in our bedroom right by me. I'm sure he could see it was bad but probably just thought it was another ol' migraine. He left for the kitchen to get me some medication. Anything to take away some of this pain, even just a little. He came back and I gave in to the nudge.

"Nate," I said, "my head hurts so bad, something's not right and I'm scared." He helped me to the bathroom and I vomited in the toilet. People throw up sometimes when they have migraines, right? Yeah, that's all this is, just a really bad migraine.

Nate called my OB doctor. We needed some guidance on how to help relieve this pressure because it wasn't letting up. Hearing only Nate's side of the conversation, I gathered that they were closed (because it was a Saturday) and the person who had answered the phone would let the on-call doctor know and he/she would give us a call back within thirty minutes. The possibility of waiting thirty minutes made my head spin all the more.

As I hunched over the toilet, I felt my fingers and toes cramp together. I couldn't straighten them and they wouldn't uncramp. *What is going on?* was all I could think. I was desperate for Nate to do something, anything. I told him I was cramping and he was immediately back on the phone with the OB.

When apparently given the same thirty-minute spiel a second time, I heard my sweet husband get frustrated with the nurse. He said, "Well, what the heck am I supposed to do until then? My wife's really not okay over here!"

I was starting to phase in and out of consciousness. I remember looking at our son, Declan, watching me from the bathroom door with this concerned look on his face. I was still hovered over the toilet and I heard Nate ask him to go play with his toys in the living room. The next thing I remember was lying on the bathroom floor and Nate asking me to raise my hands and smile at him. I did as he asked, thinking to myself, *Well, that's an odd request.*

— NATE'S STORY —

It was an odd request because my wife was oddly not raising her left arm when she was telling me she was.

I remember being quite frustrated with the nurse when she told me the on-call doctor would get back to me within half an hour the second time. Apparently, she couldn't sense the urgency of my words or the urgent way I spoke those urgent words. With our on-demand, everything-at-our-fingertips culture, I was surprised that a doctor's office would use something as antiquated as a pager. I wanted this doctor to call me back, stat!

Obviously, that wasn't going to happen. Shortly thereafter, Anna lost control of her bladder on the bathroom floor. And once Anna told me she was cramping, I hung up and called 911. I initially assumed that the cramping had something to do with the baby, which is why I called 911 right away. Later, I found out that Anna's fingers and toes were starting to curl up and cramp, most likely from the building pressure in her head.

The 911 operator immediately assessed the situation and once I mentioned that Anna's speech was a bit slurred, had me ask Anna to raise both of her arms above her head. After I realized that Anna couldn't move her left arm, the operator had me ask Anna to smile. Only the right side smiled. The only thing I could think was that my wife was having a stroke. Which doesn't happen to young people, right? What in the world is going on?

Within minutes, I heard sirens approaching. I quickly sent a text to our immediate families that read, "Anna is not doing very well, please pray! EMS is on their way."

First to arrive was an EMT with the Ottawa County Sheriff's Department. He basically took Anna's vitals and rolled her on her side as she began to vomit again.

Thankfully, my parents and Anna's dad were nearby and they were able to take our son, Declan, off of our hands. While Anna was throwing up in the bathroom, Declan kept coming in with his basketball, asking us in his broken, 1.5-year-old language for "Mommy (to) shoot hoops." It broke my heart having to sternly, and repeatedly, tell him that Mommy couldn't shoot hoops and to get out of the bathroom. I got the sense that he knew something serious was going on but had no idea what.

A few moments later, the ambulance arrived. I'll never, ever forget the sight of Anna being wheeled through our front door on a stretcher. Not an experience I'd recommend.

– ANNA'S STORY –

After Nate asking me to raise my hands, I remember nothing. I was unconscious. Everything went dark. I don't remember the ambulance or stretcher. I don't remember our parents coming to our house to take Declan or the ride to Holland Hospital. I don't remember the doctors or nurses who quickly diagnosed me with a ruptured brain aneurysm and transferred me straight to Spectrum Health in Grand Rapids. Nothing about needing a drain to relieve pressure and certainly nothing about brain surgery.

Looking back now, I know this was God's way of protecting me. Protecting our baby, (whom we later named Hudson). I didn't need to stress about what was happening. About shaving my head or what might happen during brain surgery. Stress about who had Declan or how my sweet husband and family were coping. Research shows that stress can have a detrimental effect on a developing baby. From my being unconscious the entire time, our sweet unborn boy didn't need to suffer the consequences of that stress either.

God's hand was on me and Hudson the entire time, starting from the very first twinge of pain to the gentle nudge I felt from Him to let Nate know how serious this was. He allowed the aneurysm to happen while Nate was five feet away.

I know you can go crazy thinking about the what-ifs, but I can't help but think what if all this had happened while Nate was at work or even out running an errand. I would have convinced myself it was just another migraine, definitely not worth calling Nate about. Just thinking about how quickly I deteriorated with the vomiting, then cramping, and then paralysis and eventually blacking out . . . by the time I realized what was happening it could have been too late to call him, and then . . . well, just too late.

But the nudge. Looking back, I know that was only from God. John 10:3-4 explains it perfectly. "The sheep listen to his voice. He calls his own sheep by name and leads them out . . . his sheep follow him because they know his voice." Although I was uncertain and doubted more than I'd like to admit, I knew deep down it was my Shepherd's, my Savior's voice urging me to let Nate know how serious this was. What if I hadn't listened to that still, small voice?

Thinking about the what-ifs in these cases just makes me praise God all the more. Tears run down my face as I think about just how much my heavenly Father must love me. "Look at the birds of the air: they neither sow nor reap nor gather into barns, and yet your heavenly Father feeds them. Are you not of more value than they" (Matthew 6:26, ESV).

All I can think is, *Why me? Why and how can He love me so much? I'm just a lowly sinner who He, for whatever reason, decides to forgive and love and show grace to every single day.* Undeniable, undeserving, overwhelming grace. I don't deserve a love like that. You don't deserve a love like that but He still gives the gift freely. Lord, my Lord, how majestic is your name in all the earth! Life could've turned out so differently.

Our neurosurgeon said 50 percent of those who have this type of aneurysm don't even make it to the hospital alive and the remaining 70 percent who do make it end up having mental or physical deficits afterward.

Grace, God's grace, made all the difference for me. His grace has allowed me to still be here today. To continue loving life and doing life with my marriage partner and best friend. To continue being a mommy to two of the sweetest boys I've ever laid eyes on. To go to the beach and paint my nails. To say "hi" to strangers and love the least of these. To share my story of a lowly, everyday, ordinary, stay-at-home mom to bring glory to His name. And as long as I've been given this second chance, that's exactly what I'm going to do. Make God's name great. Give hope to the hopeless. Shine His healing for the broken and, as a speaker at a conference I recently went to proclaimed, "Lord, I dare to be Your light, let my life light up the sky!" Matthew 5:14-16 says this: "You are the light of the world. A city on a hill cannot be hidden. Neither do people light a lamp and put it under a basket. Instead, they set it on a lampstand, and it gives light to everyone in the house. In the same way, let your light shine before men, that they may see your good deeds and glorify your Father in heaven."

This is my purpose, my passion, and for those who are followers of Christ . . . it should be yours too. It doesn't need to take a brain aneurysm or a close brush with death to make that your passion. In fact, I pray that is not the case! We are called to be light to this broken and hurting world. I pray that during the events, circumstances, and situations we find ourselves in, whether big or small, we would always turn the spotlight back to Him. To the one who makes all things new in His time. To the one who is on the throne forever and ever. To the one who orchestrates and allows the good and bad events in our life to happen. To our healer, protector, sustainer, and provider. To our good, good Father. Because if we do this, and do it well, we can be a small piece of Jesus to a world that so desperately needs Him. I pray that as you read our story you will see our Father's good deeds and glorify Him too!

Journey with us through this story. Our story. Share in our highs and our lows. Experience the miracles with us again. There are many, and we can't wait to share with the world how great our God is. Walk with us as we recall and relive some of the most terrifying, uncertain, faith-building days of our lives. Walk with us through 18 days of grace.

— NATE'S STORY —

I'll never forget the words the doctor told me in the ER at Holland Hospital. "Nate, the CT scan shows that your wife has suffered from a subarachnoid hemorrhage, or ruptured brain aneurysm."

Umm . . . excuse me, what?

I remember being at a complete loss as to what to think, or even feel. I understood, to some extent, the gravity of the situation but

Nate Weeber with <u>Anna Weeber</u>.

September 10, 2016 · Holland

URGENT!! To all PRAYER WARRIORS - Anna has had a severe aneurism and will shortly be going from Holland Hospital to GR. Please pray to the God of Miracles that my wife, best friend, lover and soulmate will be restored to full health! Your prayers are coveted!!

<u>162 others like this</u>   263 shares

could not wrap my mind around the fact that my perfectly healthy, twenty-seven-year-old wife had a ruptured brain aneurysm. Aren't those just for old people? Or at least unhealthy people? Psalm 23 talks about walking through the valley, and this was a deep one for me. Anna's parents were with us in the ER, but I remember feeling so alone and heavily burdened—like someone had put a two hundred-pound pack on my shoulders and I immediately had to carry it until whatever this thing was was over. My mind was racing with questions that I didn't know whom to ask. Was Anna going to be paralyzed on the left side for good? How can she function as a mom this way? Would she need a wheelchair? Is our baby okay? Is there an insurance that covers something like this? Do we even have it? The woman who I share everything with—from my biggest joys to my deepest, darkest secrets—was lying unconscious on a hospital bed. I was holding her hand, but it felt like she was miles away. I wanted so desperately to talk to her, to hold her and tell her how scared I was.

Nate Weeber with Anna Weeber.

September 10, 2016 · Holland

Flying down the road in an ambulance, sirens blaring on our way to GR. This is absolutely surreal. Our God is Healer and He has a plan but BOY is this tough! Thanks so much for your texts/messages, etc, and especially your prayers! GOD IS GOOD ALL THE TIME

117 others like this   12 shares

Well, this was just nuts. I still couldn't believe it. Am I really flying down the road in an ambulance with my half-paralyzed, pregnant wife lying in the back, unconscious on a stretcher? Weren't we just watching a football game and about to go for a bike ride? I tried to make small talk with the driver, but it was tough. Mostly about other patients they had had in the past and that sort of thing.

By the way, our EMTs were nothing short of John Cena's twin and Barbie on steroids. He may as well have carried us all there on his back and gotten us there just as quickly and safely. And I'm pretty sure she moonlit as a personal trainer. Of herself. When they weren't in the ambulance, I'm guessing they spent a fair amount of time at the gym. And Twinkies were definitely not in their diet. Folks, we had the A-Team.

— ANNA'S STORY —

Being completely out of it the day of the rupture, I can't add much detail besides what people tell me. In case you're like me, you may be wondering, *What even is a ruptured brain aneurysm?* An aneurysm is a balloon-like bulge of an artery wall. As an aneurysm grows, it puts pressure on nearby structures and may eventually rupture. A ruptured aneurysm releases blood into the spaces around the brain, and it's called a subarachnoid hemorrhage, a life-threatening type of stroke.

One of Nate's friends who works as a nurse in Holland Hospital wrote Nate a few days later, saying she has never witnessed such a quick turnaround of diagnosing and getting a patient off to Spectrum. The aneurysm that I had was very severe, and being twenty-six weeks pregnant on top of that made for the perfect storm. I am so grateful to all the amazing doctors and nurses at Holland Hospital. To the sweet nurse who prayed with my weeping, overwhelmed mom, to the doctors who diagnosed me so quickly, to the ambulance drivers who got me safely and quickly to Spectrum.

Throughout the whole experience, doctors kept saying to us, "Time is brain." Meaning, the quicker they could fix the problem or recognize the warning signs, the more brain they could save and the better off I would be. God placed exactly the right doctors and nurses at exactly the right time so I could have the very best (and quickest) care possible.

Fast-forward six months after this was all said and done when my mom coincidentally saw the ER doctor from Holland Hospital at a funeral and asked if he by chance remembered either of us. He said that he certainly did and he had been keeping up with our story and praying for us! Then he said something that shakes me. He said, "I really didn't think she was going to make it." I shudder thinking how close I was to death. How close I was to not ever going out on another date with Nate or watching Declan play in his first soccer game.

Yet it compels me and encourages me in a way like no other that God still has a purpose for me on this earth and He needs me to complete it. One of my very favorite verses in the Bible before the aneurysm is found in Esther and I believe it's even more applicable after having the aneurysm. It says, "And who knows whether you have not come to the kingdom for such a time as this?" Mordecai was urging Esther that maybe she had been put in her position as queen for a very specific purpose at a very specific time—to save her people.

I truly believe God allowed this to happen to me for a very specific purpose at a very specific time. Even if this book or our story encourages or brings hope to just one person, it will all have been worth it. God has used and continues to use our story more than we ever thought possible. He is using it for a specific purpose and we are humbled and honored to be a part of His story.

DAY 1

*"Before I was born, God chose me
and called me by His marvelous Grace."*

GALATIANS 1:15

Nate Weeber with <u>Anna Weeber</u>.

September 11, 2016 · Grand Rapids

Update: Anna has officially had a brain aneurysm. She will most likely be having a tube inserted into her brain within the next hour or two to stabilize pressure from the blood that is now in her brain (Forgive me for my lack of medical knowledge). She will be having brain surgery tomorrow morning at 7:30am to put a clamp on the spot that has had the aneurysm. 3-4 hour surgery.

8 hours ago Anna and I got Dec up from a nap after watching U of M destroy UCF and were planning on going on a bike ride with Dec. If you had told me 8 hours ago that I would have seen my 27 yr-old, vibrant, full-of-life wife limp on her left side (which has thankfully now come back), taken into an ambulance in a stretcher from our house, rushed to the hospital in GR and now getting ready for brain surgery, I would have told you that you were crazy. I absolutely can't wrap my mind around it. One of the neurosurgeons said 50% of the people that have these don't even make it to the hospital so I am incredibly grateful that she is as good as she is. She's in a ton of pain, exhausted and in and out of it but beneath it all I can tell that friendly, bubbly Anna that we all love is still in there.

Please, please pray that Anna's body will respond well to everything that will be happening with the procedures. Little baby boy #2 is doing well right now, but there is a risk that he might have to come out early with the trauma from the surgery tomorrow morning. Please pray that he will stay in there and be as happy and healthy as can be.

I honestly can't believe that I'm typing any of this and I don't even know how to process my thoughts or emotions other than giving it to my heavenly Papa. I'm so at a loss for words but I'm feeling His arms (and yours) wrapped tightly around us. I usually have Anna at my side for tough stuff like this, but maybe God is teaching me to rely on Him more. Your prayers are GREATLY appreciated. I'm so thankful for all of your encouraging texts, FB messages, calls, etc.

Please keep praying. I know God will be glorified through this (and I want Him to be) but that doesn't mean it's easy (this absolutely sucks right now). The body of Christ is such an amazing thing and I am so grateful for each one of you.

Nate

<u>272 others like this</u> <u>285 shares</u>

1

– ANNA'S STORY –

The pressure was still unbelievable. So many doctors and nurses coming in and out of the room. People crying. So many people crying. Neurologists and nurses were constantly asking me the same questions. "What month is it? Who is the president? What state do you live in? Where are you now?"

"September, Barack Obama, Michigan, Spectrum Health." I was nailing these questions, which was a good sign. Nate had left the hospital to run home and grab a quick shower before returning. My mom and mother-in-law were in the room with me when yet another nurse came in and began asking me the same questions.

"What month is it?" "Sandy Pines" was my answer.

"What state do you live in?" "Apple Crisp."

Our moms looked at each other with dismay and tears in their eyes.

"No, try again," they said to the nurse. "She just got the questions right moments before."

The pressure was getting to be too much. My blood-filled, over-pressurized brain started to affect my cognitive abilities. This was the exact reason they asked these questions so often. To tell when or if *this* started happening. My mother-in-law quickly texted Nate and told him the doctor wanted to insert a drain into my brain to relieve some of the pressure, right away.

I still remember none of this. This same day I was wheeled into surgery. My family didn't know if that would be the last time they saw me alive. My husband was warned that they might have to take our baby boy out early if he became distressed. I think back to what that must have been like for them. How hard it must have been. Sometimes I think that they had it worse than I did—since I was unconscious so much of the time, I really didn't know what all was happening.

I absolutely love how God works. My neurosurgeon, Dr. Justin Singer, was a newer addition to the Spectrum team who was and is phenomenal at what he does. His wife just so happened to be one week behind me in her pregnancy. He really took us under his wing and treated me like he would have his own wife at this stage in pregnancy. I know it gave Nate so much peace. Dr. Singer told us multiple times that when he had to make decisions regarding my care, he would think about what he would want done to his own wife and child. Even the fact that Dr. Singer cared so much about our little boy, not believing he was just a "sack of tissue" like many others believe in this day and age, was another example of God's sovereignty.

This was not just luck or a funny coincidence. This was yet one more example of God at work. Caring about even the little details that He knew would give my husband and family peace. Caring for the least of these.

— NATE'S STORY —

Time just dragged by. Doctors kept filtering in and out of the room, hooking up various bags of medication, checking vitals, and asking Anna a routine set of questions to test her brain function. If the pressure got too great, they would need to drill a hole in the top of Anna's head and insert a shunt to drain blood and excess brain fluid. Typically, the head regulates this pressure on its own, but people usually lose this function with a brain trauma.

They asked Anna a set of four to six questions every twenty minutes for hours. For the first 10 or so hours, she did very well and accurately answered the questions every time.

Thankfully, we had quite a few visitors come to the hospital to see how Anna was doing during this time; mainly family at this point and a few pastors from our home church. It was so encouraging that they all took the time to come and see us, and it was a nice distraction from what was going on.

After about nine hours of hanging out while the doctors were doing their thing, I decided to drive home quickly to take a shower and pick up a few things for the hospital. While I was in the shower, I heard a text come through on my phone. Do you ever have it when you hear your phone ring and you know who is calling? When I heard my phone go off, I knew it wasn't good. Of course, it was 4:20 a.m., so it obviously had something to do with Anna. The text was from my mom, and it read, "Nate, Dr. feels it's necessary to do drain soon . . . will start in 5-10 mins."

I quickly got dressed, grabbed a few things, and flew back to the hospital. I'm not really sure why; I knew the procedure would take an hour and a half, and it only takes twenty-five minutes to get to Spectrum, but there's something comforting about being closer to a loved one when they go through something like this. When I walked into the lobby of Anna's floor, I saw both of our moms deep in prayer together, holding hands. There were quite a few silver linings to this whole experience, and this was one of them for me. A pretty neat thing for a son to see. Our families on both sides are such a blessing to us, and we are so thankful for our shared faith.

After another hour, one of Anna's doctors came into the lobby with a smile on his face—the procedure had gone swimmingly. Praise the Lord!

Nate Weeber

September 11, 2016 · Grand Rapids

Update: Anna was just wheeled into surgery. Can't wait to see her when she's out. Please pray hard for Anna, baby and the surgeon and everybody else in that room! Our God is the Great Physician and I can't wait for good news. Will keep you posted. God is Good.

106 Comments   250 others like this   55 Shares

— NATE'S STORY —

I'll never forget the final minutes before Anna was wheeled into surgery. It was one of those moments where you feel like you're about to be pushed off a cliff. It's inevitable, and it has to be done, but you don't know if there's a pool of water at the bottom or a slab of concrete. Every word of love and devotion that we expressed to each other in those final moments was so tangible I could almost taste them coming out of my mouth.

I've found that I generally like to be in control of things in life. And I think most people do. This. Was. Tough. The longest three hours of my life.

There were about thirty people who came to hang out during the surgery—mostly family, but a few close friends and respected people from the community stopped by as well.

— ANNA'S STORY —

I later found out that on this day—this scary, uncertain, momentous day—there was a rainbow. And not just a rainbow, but a double rainbow. My dad posted on Facebook: "Standing on the Promises!! If you look close—there are two rainbows—one for Anna, and a little one for baby. God is so good!!" I didn't know about it then, but I didn't need to. I believe God placed those rainbows in the sky on that day to encourage my family. To remind them of God's faithfulness. Of His promises. Of His love. No, we didn't know my outcome or even how the next few hours would go, but we knew God was with us. We knew His will would be done. We knew we had the promise of eternity no matter how things went in that operating room. We knew God's name would be glorified even if my physical outcome wasn't what we hoped for.

Nate Weeber with Anna Weeber.

September 11, 2016 · Grand Rapids

Surgery update: just got a call that everything is going well and on track! Still working their way to the aneurysm. Having some sweet, sweet times of prayer at the hospital. This is tough, but God is Good.

I'm blown away and humbled by all of the kindness and encouragement. Love you all.

And thank you all so much for your prayers! Please keep it up.

"Where prayer is focused, Power falls" - Mike Faris

301 others like this   66 Comments   66 Shares

Nate Weeber with <u>Anna Weeber</u>.

September 11, 2016 · Grand Rapids

Surgery update #2: Doc says everything is going smoothly - aneurysm has been successfully clamped and the surgeon is starting to close things up! God is Good. Please pray things continue to go well!

<u>371 others like this</u> <u>75 Comments</u> <u>88 Shares</u>

Nate Weeber with <u>Anna Weeber</u>.

September 11, 2016 · Grand Rapids

Final surgery update: surgery went PERFECTLY WELL! Aneurysm is clamped and I haven't seen my bride yet but she is in recovery and hopefully resting as comfortably as she can. Friends, we serve a BIG GOD. And for some reason, He loves and cares for us like we're his own kids. Because we are. Unbelievable.

Please continue to pray for Anna's weeks-long recovery process at the hospital and the months to follow at home. She has a number of hurdles to jump yet with recovery.

I am truly, truly humbled by the outpouring of intercession on our behalf and love towards us over the past 20 hours. We are SO blessed to call you our family and our friends.

I'll continue to keep you updated, but right now it's time to see my babe.

<u>648 others like this</u> <u>141 Comments</u> <u>205 Shares</u>

— NATE'S STORY —

I couldn't wait to see Anna. The last time I saw her, she was floating back and forth between extreme pain and sleeping. I was able to ask her a few questions here and there, but nothing substantial enough to know whether she was truly aware of the gravity of the situation and everything that was taking place. And what is someone like after brain surgery? Are they the same?

The lobby was filled with friends and family, but I got to go see my bride alone. I wound my way through the halls to her room, almost giddy with excitement. I wanted to run, but I didn't think the ICU was the best place to work on my cardio.

I walked in the room and there she was. The most beautiful woman I've ever seen. And she had a big smile on her face! She was alert as can be and had a very low level of pain. I don't think I've ever felt as much relief in my life. It had only been twenty hours since this whole thing started, and it was so good to have her back.

Our conversation consisted mostly of talking about what had happened from my perspective and hers. I don't know how many times I said, "Anna. You just had brain surgery. *Brain. Surgery.*" Followed by laughter, almost out of disbelief. After about ten minutes of basking in her presence (including conversation and many kisses), I walked back to the lobby and announced, "She's back!"

DAY 2

*"Every weakness you have is an opportunity for God
to show His strength in your life."*

2 CORINTHIANS 12:9 (personal paraphrase)

Nate Weeber with Anna Weeber.

September 12, 2016 · Grand Rapids

Recovery update: Anna is doing very well. She is quite tired and has a pretty bad headache, both of which are expected, but said her pain is now at a 4/10 today compared to a 5-6/10 yesterday after surgery and a 9/10 when we first brought her in. So thankful for that! Can't wait until that 4 is a 0, Lord willing.

Anna is expected to be in the ICU at Spectrum in GR for 2-3 weeks. It will probably /hopefully be on the 2-week side because of her young age and good health.

She is currently in the Honeymoon stage of her recovery, which is the first 3-5 days when Anna will most likely be doing quite well. The neurosurgeon said some "storm clouds" may start to roll in around days 5-7 with potential complications due to the draining blood from her brain, etc, but they continue to monitor her every hour to watch for issues to arise. Please pray hard that those storm clouds just don't show up.

Baby #2 is doing remarkably well. There was a somewhat decent chance they would have to remove him during the surgery yesterday via C-section, but he did great. Baby's heartbeat was monitored during the surgery and at one point they didn't think they could hear it and had to ultrasound to find it because his and Anna's heartbeats were in sink. The maternity Dr. who is currently watching over the baby said they are only going to check on him once a day now instead of the planned 2x a day because he is doing so well. For a while there I thought I might be splitting my time between the ICU and the neonatal unit and I'm praising Jesus that isn't the case. Just got to hear the heartbeat for 20 minutes and it is nice and strong.

Both Anna and baby are being extremely well taken care of at Spectrum Butterworth. We are blessed to be so close to one of the top hospitals in the country.

The messages I have received from people all over the US and the world (China, Romania, Italy, France, Canada) have been so genuinely encouraging. With stories like - family friends of ours that live near us in Holland were out of town over the weekend (hours away from us) and they found out about Anna's aneurysm because someone else at this church they were visiting asked the church to pray for Nate and Anna Weeber. Blows my mind! People around the country have been telling me their whole church is praying for Anna, from Georgia to Washington and everywhere in between.

Your love and compassion for Anna and me has been truly touching. Your level of concern is so humbling to both of us. Our God is so good no matter the outcome and as unusual and trying as these next months will probably be. Please keep praying for a continued strong recovery.

Love you all! Nate

678 others like this   105 Comments   169 Shares

9

– ANNA'S STORY –

Can I just take a minute to state how amazing my husband is? As he's sitting in the ambulance not sure if his wife is going to make it, he's writing things like, "God is good all the time." This man amazes me. His faith not once wavered through all of this. His trust in God during this time is something I will never forget. I look up to him and respect him so much and can't help but think, *If I was put in his shoes, would my faith be that strong? Would I be able to handle thinking I may have to plan a funeral but still proclaim that God is good and has a purpose in this all?* This man drives me to want to be a better person, a better wife, a better follower of Christ every day. I am truly undeserving of this man God has blessed me with.

I get choked up when I think about these next two things. One, during the surgery they were consistently monitoring Hudson to make sure his heart was beating strong and he wasn't getting too stressed. At one point, they couldn't find our sweet boy's heartbeat. Just hearing those words break my heart. But then, finding out that after they rushed in an ultrasound machine, the reason they couldn't hear his heartbeat was because it was perfectly in sync with mine. That just makes my heart burst with an amount of love for this little boy I don't even know how to describe. This, to me, is just one more touch from God saying, "Don't worry . . . I've got both of you in my hands. You are *My* children, and I love you both more than you can imagine."

The second thing that gets me choked up is hearing from Nate after the surgery how many people, how many of *you* were praying for us. The number of people that somehow heard about our story and began praying is astronomical. People all over the world. I have never felt so humbled and so undeserving of anything in my life. I am amazed and so grateful for the body of Christ. I have no doubt that the prayers that were sent up had a direct impact on how the rest of my hospital stay went as well as the rest of my outcome. God used all these prayer warriors to tangibly show us His love, His power, and His healing. When we were at our weakest, He became the strongest. Second Corinthians 12:9 tells us, "But he said to me, 'My grace is sufficient for you, for my power is made perfect in weakness. Therefore I will boast all the more gladly about my weaknesses, so that Christ's power may rest on me.'" Showing weakness or sickness isn't a negative thing; it's an opportunity for God to show up. An opportunity for God to show us His strength.

— NATE'S STORY —

During this time, I received hundreds upon hundreds of text and Facebook messages, a lot of which began with something like, "Hi Nate, you don't know me, but I came across your story and wanted to let you know that my family and I are praying for complete healing for Anna" from (fill in the blank). Mostly from people in the United States, but also from Germany, Romania, China, Italy, France, and Africa. It was humbling to think that people all over the globe were lifting my wife up in prayer at all times of the day in different time zones (and maybe even different languages). Keep in mind, the following does not at all fit correct theology of God being right here with us, but I get a picture in my mind of God looking down at earth and seeing/hearing all of these prayers come up to Him like little light beams.

One of those messages was from someone that neither Anna nor I know:

"Hello Nate. We don't know each other, but between your wife and yourself we have a few mutual friends and I have been following your story and praying for you guys. I wanted to share a little story that happened this morning. I do online customer service for a retail company based in Colorado. This morning when replying to a customer complaint I entered the woman's name into our system (her name was Susan S.) and hit enter. While waiting for her profile to load I switched tabs and was looking at Facebook. I read your prayer request that you posted this morning. I stopped there and prayed. I then went back to my customer profile window and the name that was showing was 'Anna Heal.' I had a few different windows going with different things but could not figure out where I had pulled this name from. Then it hit me . . . God is a miracle worker and He is the ultimate great physician. Keep trusting, and I will keep praying! May the Lord bless you and your wife (and your boys)!!"

Wow. I still remember sitting in the chair next to Anna when I read this message. I am absolutely floored at how sovereign our God is. And not only that, but how deeply involved He is in our lives on a very personal level. This whole experience brought me a much greater understanding of the direct and almost tangible workings God is always doing in our lives. He is *always* at work, but it's simply more evident to us if we're looking for it with expectation.

Nate Weeber with Anna Weeber.

September 12, 2016 · Ottawa Center

Monday night update: Thank you all so much for your prayers! God has graciously allowed Anna to continue recovering well for now. A Speech Therapist visited the room today and went through a bunch of cognitive exercises with Anna and she did very, very well. A Physical Therapist and Occupational Therapist came in as well and checked out her motor skills, etc. I couldn't believe it when they asked her if she wanted to try standing up! And then they took her for a walk down the hallway! I couldn't believe it.

Within 48 hours, Anna has had a serious brain aneurysm, was completely limp on her left side, had brain surgery, and is back up walking. Folks, if that's not miraculous, I don't know what is! I am beyond blown away by God's grace in Anna's recovery.

Your prayers and encouragement are such a blessing to both of us. Your messages and comments often brings tears to my eyes when I think about the fact that you're taking the time to check up on us.

Anna is still very exhausted, as can be expected, but the nurses have to walk through certain cognitive and physical exercises every hour 24/7 for the next two weeks to make sure she isn't having any complications. Please pray that she'll be able to sleep soundly in between.

"Do not fear, for I am with you;
do not be afraid, for I am your God.
I will strengthen you;
I will help you;
I will hold on to you with my righteous right hand." Isaiah 41:10

Boom. Those are some good words right there. Keep praying!

Love you all. Nate

608 others like this   114 Comments   130 Shares

— ANNA'S STORY —

Walking! I was walking. I had to will my legs to move, and it felt like two hundred-pound weights were chained to both of my ankles, but I was walking! I was beating the odds with every step I took. I think of Peter stepping out of the boat to meet Jesus. How scary this must have been—but he did it! He walked on water! Until he began to doubt, until he took his eyes off his Savior, freaked out, and started sinking because of it.

During this whole ordeal, God not only saved my life, He allowed us to be free from doubt. Nate and I had faith that God would work this out for His good, no matter my outcome. I don't say this to brag or to make you think I'm "better than" because that is far from the truth. But this is just one more way, one more miracle that God used by allowing us to remain strong in our faith. I don't know how we would've gotten through without our faith in Him. Without our prayer warriors lifting us up. Often we would get Facebook messages from people saying they were awakened in the middle of the night only to get down on their knees and pray for us.

People, God wasn't only working in *our* lives and on *our* behalf. He was working in those faithful servants, those prayer warriors too. He was increasing *all* of our faith; He was bringing hope to *all* the hopeless; He was displaying miracles for *all* to see; and He was teaching us *all* a very important lesson. God's grace can conquer the statistics, it can defy the odds, it can stun the doctors, and it can cover a couple in such a tangible way, they go away praising God for all the things they have seen and heard.

DAY 3

"Then he touched their eyes and said,
'According to your faith let it be done to you.'"

MATTHEW 9:29

Nate Weeber

September 13, 2016 · Grand Rapids

Tuesday afternoon update: God is good - Anna continues to do well. She is still about the same, pain-wise and everything. The drainage from her brain through the shunt is starting to slow down a bit, which is exactly what the Drs want to have happen.

Anna is starting to get into the "storm cloud" range, and they are watching out for Vasospasms. This is when blood vessels in the head get irritated from the blood drainage and spasm/constrict and shut off blood flow to parts of her brain. Please pray for no Vasospasms and that God keeps those blood vessels wide open.

As I am typing this, a nurse just told Anna that now that they have the blood in her brain under control (praise the Lord), they need to watch out for blood clots in her legs. Please pray that no clots will develop.

I can't imagine what Anna is really thinking and feeling through all of this. Please pray for God's peace and contentment for her. It seems like she has a lot of it and is happy as she can be, but it has got to be tough. She has told me a number of times that she can't wait to get back home and get back to normal.

Anna is taking a brief snooze before she has to take medication at 2pm. Hillsong Worship is softly playing on Pandora a few feet from her bed. Good Good Father just came on. If you haven't heard it before, take a listen.

God is so good.

Thanks so much, everybody. Love you all!

Nate

Chris Tomlin—Good Good Father
(Lyrics And Chords)

M.YOUTUBE.COM

362 others like this   55 Comments   67 Shares

Nate Weeber with Anna Weeber.

September 13, 2016 · Grand Rapids

Tuesday night update: More great news! Anna was very happy to hear that the nurses will be doing the neuro-exam every 4 hours now instead of every 1 hour because she is doing so well! This means Anna gets to SLEEP! They will still be giving her medication every 2 hours to reduce the chance of Vasospasms, but that is just a quick pill and some water. They will also be doing an ultrasound of her brain every morning to make sure that her blood vessels aren't constricting at all and blood flow is normal.

Little baby is doing very well also. Happy and content. They are not giving Anna anything for the baby, other than additional nutrition, and continue to monitor him every day.

Please continue to pray that the blood vessels in Anna's brain continue to function properly and that she doesn't get any blood clots in her legs. Please also pray that if any of the above does occur that the doctors and nurses will be able to catch it quickly and resolve the issue.

This whole entire process has so clearly been Father Filtered. I could go on for a VERY long time about all of the details that God had obviously lined up before the aneurysm even began! Way cool. We've got a BIG God who cares about even the smallest detail!

One of those little details: I am sitting at McDonalds across the street from the hospital with my brother, Mark, as I type this. For "some reason" the conference he was supposed to be at in Dallas right now got postponed a couple of days and his work schedule is very flexible this week (normally it isn't) so he high-tailed it for Michigan on Sunday. Undeserving of a brother like him and thankful God paved the way for him to be here!

Each one of you is such an encouragement to us in your own way, even if not intentionally. I saw pictures today of the pyramids from Heather Clark Echols in Egypt and was reminded of God's faithfulness in leading the Israelites through the desert and humbled that that same powerful God is next to us holding our hands through ours. Wow.

Thank you so much for your prayers - Keep expectantly praying for big things!! God is listening. Please also pray that we will gladly accept whatever God's will is in the long run. I absolutely want my bride to be healed 100%, and healed soon, but I want God to get glory and use this in whatever way He sees fit, as hard is that is to even say.

We both appreciate you all so much!

Love you all!

Nate

527 others like this   50 Comments   82 Shares

– ANNA'S STORY –

As I read this post from Nate, I am in awe when he says, "I absolutely want my bride to be healed 100 percent, and healed soon, but I want God to get glory and use this in whatever way He sees fit, as hard is that is to even say."

Again, no words necessary except Thank You, Father, for this amazing, godly, faith-filled man. I seriously can't believe he's *my* husband. I. Am. Blessed.

Trying to eat at the hospital was getting to be tough. I couldn't chew crunchy or hard foods because it hurt my jaw so much. Dr. Singer had to move around some muscles by my ear after making the incision to get where he needed to in my brain. The incision went just in front of my right ear all the way up to the top of my head. This forced me to be on an almost all-liquid diet of smoothies, mashed potatoes, applesauce, and yogurt. I didn't feel hungry much, and the few calories I was getting weren't very substantial. The nurses came in frequently, always trying to get me to eat more. Food really didn't sound good most of the time, but I remember forcing myself to eat for Hudson's sake, knowing he needed calories and good nutrition to keep growing and developing at a healthy rate. This was probably the *one* time during both of my pregnancies where food didn't sound good or I didn't feel like I could eat a small village. Miracles do happen, folks!

DAY 4

Now all glory to God, who is able,
through his mighty power at work within us,
to accomplish infinitely more than we might ask or think.

EPHESIANS 3:20 (NLT)

Nate Weeber with Anna Weeber.

September 14, 2016 · Grand Rapids

Wednesday afternoon update: A heartfelt thank you to all of you for your continued prayers and encouragement. God's presence has been very tangible to me through this entire process and I can feel His family lifting us up. Please pray that it is felt just as strongly for Anna as well. Hard to know exactly what she is feeling emotionally and experiencing with all of the pain meds and everything. God continues to amaze us!

Four (more) praise items: 1 - Both of Anna's pupils have been the same dilation now for a day which is a very good sign. One was more dilated than the other for a few days, but both are looking great now. 2 - When the nurses have been testing the strength of her legs/feet every hour, her left had been weaker than the right but both are now the same. 3 - The right side of her face had been swelling a fair amount which is normal and expected from the surgery, so she hadn't been able to open her right eye nearly as much as her left. I was happily surprised when I walked in this morning to see both eyes opened almost the same width! 4 - Anna just took another walk down the hall and walked twice as far as she did two days ago. It's very exhausting for her, but so good to see how quickly she is improving! Bless God for His goodness!

A LOT of people have been asking how they can help. Your generosity and concern even for me through this process has been very touching. A meal-train is being set up through our church, First Baptist of Zeeland, and I think some of Anna's cousins are making some frozen meals as well which will be VERY helpful as we transition home in the coming weeks, Lord willing.

Other than that we are being very well taken care of right now. My parents and Anna's parents are taking care of Declan for now and all of the logistics behind that which has been a very helpful. He is absolutely loving it. He visited a little while ago and got to lay next to mommy while she read a book to him for a very short time. Anna is the best mommy I could ever imagine our kid(s) having. I am so undeserving to have her as my partner as a parent and wife!

I know I've said this many times before but God has provided for our every need. Anna had cleaned our house and done laundry on Friday, the day before this happened. We bought a chest freezer about a month ago that is sitting in our basement completely empty so we now have plenty of space for freezer meals. "When I think of the wisdom and scope of God's plan, I fall to my knees and pray to the Father, the Creator of everything in heaven and on earth" (Eph. 3:14). EVERY detail has been planned out and taken care of by our Provider and it is so obvious! I'm thankful God has allowed me/us to see Him so clearly holding our hands through all of this.

Please continue to pray that God keeps Anna's blood vessels from constricting and for no blood clots. Please also pray for rest and comfort for Anna in between all of the medications, shots, poking and prodding. She is such a trooper and has such a good attitude! I haven't heard her complain ONCE. Baby is still happy and content but please continue praying for him as well and that none of the medications or radiation they are using will have a negative effect on his development.

God is so good and so faithful. I don't know what the final outcome will be, but I know He is with us and He's got it all taken care of. I know I'm a fairly simple guy and it doesn't take much to impress me but I am still BLOWN AWAY by our Heavenly Papa and all of you.

"Now glory be to God! By his mighty power at work within us, he is able to accomplish infinitely more than we would ever dare to ask or hope." Eph. 3:20

Keep expectantly praying for big things!

Love you all!

Nate

— ANNA'S STORY —

I can't help but read this post and think, *I must have really looked like quite something!* My pupils dilated to different sizes, the left side of my face swollen, and my eye unable to open all the way! I'm thankful Declan (or anyone else for that matter) still recognized me! As Nate had mentioned, emotionally we were both doing so well. We both had peace that truly passes all understanding; you can hear it and feel it in Nate's Facebook posts.

We were being so well taken care of. Our families visited almost every single day, taking Nate out to lunch or dinner, bringing us anything we needed, bringing Declan up to see his mommy and daddy. We were completely blown away by the doctors and nurses. Never had I witnessed (I had never had to before) just how much they do for their patients. Every single one of them was so friendly and genuinely cared about how I was doing and my comfort. The various doctors, specialists, and nurses had bedside manners that were second to none—we really felt like we were family by the end of all this. Between sponge baths and trips to the bathroom, I felt like these sweet people knew me on an entirely new and intimate level. Maybe more intimate than I'd prefer, but still. They gave me meds, tested my strength and cognitive abilities for hours on end, helped me walk, and cleaned up my vomit that at one point had literally gone all over the floor. Their jobs are tiring and endless and probably not always the most fun, but I hope every nurse out there knows how much we appreciate them. My hair had gotten to be a tangled, matted mess at this point from the drain being put in, brain surgery, not washing it, lying on it all day, etc. One sweet nurse even brushed my hair out for me, sprayed dry shampoo in it, and braided it!

These people were truly servants and excelled at their job of being hospitable, kind, and helpful. I could never thank these doctors and nurses enough for everything they did for us. They are a huge part of the reason I am as well as I am today.

Nate Weeber with Anna Weeber.

September 14, 2016 · Grand Rapids

Wednesday night update: I just asked Anna where her pain is at, and she said "it's not even a 1/10 and then said she doesn't really have a headache." Wow! Praise the Lord!

Anna had a bit of a fever this evening but it came back down not too long ago. The nurses said it could be from an infection somewhere in her body. Please pray that God will keep her infection-free!

I'm putting another song on this post. It's funny, I never really cared much for this song before, but now the words fit perfectly for where we're at.

Thank you for your continued prayers. Anna's still at a risk for Vasospasms and blood clots in her legs, so please keep praying those away.

"Don't worry about anything; instead, pray about everything. Tell God what you need and thank him for all he has done. If you do this, you will experience God's peace, which is far more wonderful than the human mind can understand." Phil. 4:6-7

Amen!

Love you all! Nate

 Oceans (Where Feet May Fail) - Hillsong United - Lyrics - Zion 2013

M.YOUTUBE.COM

289 others like this   18 Comments   35 Shares

DAY 5

He said to her, "Daughter, your faith has healed you.
Go in peace and be freed from your suffering."

MARK 5:34

Nate Weeber with Anna Weeber.

September 15, 2016 · Grand Rapids

Thursday afternoon update: PRAYER REQUEST - Anna's doctors discovered a little bit of a spasming occurring in one of Anna's blood vessels. Please pray hard that the spasming will stop immediately and the there won't be any negative side effects to her brain or body from this! Her brain has also been putting out a fair amount more fluid than it had before which isn't necessarily a bad sign, but something they are watching closely. Please pray hard that her brain will get those fluids under control.

Our God is BIG and He is Healer! Ask BOLDLY and EXPECTANTLY!!

Love you all! Nate

260 others like this   82 Comments   112 Shares

Nate Weeber with Anna Weeber.

September 15, 2016 · Grand Rapids

Thursday night update: One of Anna's doctors tonight said again that this was a significant, significant event but that she's looking like a rose. Non-Doctor Translation: Anna's aneurysm was very, very serious but she is doing incredibly well! There is SO much to praise God for! I obviously have nothing to benchmark this experience to, so it is very encouraging to me when medical staff who are familiar with this say how remarkably well Anna is doing. God is working miracle after miracle!

The "spasming" (and I hope you're not picturing Anna laying in bed having physical spasms, this is all inside her head) is very minor at this point with no physical deficiencies - think stroke-like symptoms - which is what they are concerned about. This would show that part of her brain isn't getting sufficient blood.

After a conversation with Anna's neurosurgeon, they have a very specific plan in place to get those blood vessels opened up in the event that any do seriously constrict. This usually happens anywhere from days 3-10, and today was day 5, so we're right in the middle of it. Day 7 (Saturday) is sort of a "peak" day.

Baby is still looking good!

PRAYER REQUESTS:
1 - Please pray that Anna's blood will continue to flow well to/in her brain and that there won't be lack of blood to ANY part of her brain.

23

2 - Please pray that medical staff will quickly detect and respond immediately to any deficiencies that may arise. I've heard this week a lot that "Time is Brain". The quicker they catch issues the less potential for loss of brain function.

3 - Anna is starting to get pretty uncomfortable in bed and can't imagine being able to fall asleep tonight. Her lower back, specifically, is aching quite a bit. Pray that God will help her to forget the pain and sleep deeply tonight.

4 - Pray for unwavering faith for Anna, myself and YOURSELF in Anna's healing. Mark 5:21-43 tells a powerful story of two people who were healed by faith. The second of which was a woman with a 12-year-long hemorrhage. Hmmm. Anna's type of aneurysm is termed a "subarachnoid hemorrhage". In faith, this woman touched the fringe of Jesus' robe and was immediately healed. Jesus later said to her, "Daughter, your faith has made you well. Go in peace. You have been healed."

I am praying in Jesus powerful name, a name that is above EVERY OTHER NAME, that Anna will grab the fringe of Jesus' robe in faith and be immediately healed!

"If you sinful people know how to give good gifts to your children, how much more will your Heavenly Father give good gifts to those who ask him." Matt. 7:11

We are clinging to that promise!

Anna and I had to miss the first softball game of the season tonight with our family team in a league organized by Winning At Home. We were surprised to get this picture with the recently updated team name of WEeber ARE FAMILY!

The amount of support we are getting is phenomenal.

We truly appreciate your prayers. God is hearing and is acting upon His will. Keep praying for my gorgeous bride to be healed and for His name to continue being glorified!

Love you all.

Nate

429 others like this   40 Comments   80 shares

— ANNA'S STORY —

Uncomfortable couldn't even begin to describe it. My back, my butt—everything hurt from just sitting in the same bed day in and day out. I could sit in the chair if I wanted to for a bit, but it was just so exhausting getting there. I felt so restricted and at times I just wanted to cry. Being pregnant can at times be uncomfortable enough, but then add to it needing to lie in the same bed for hours and days on end? I have a whole new level of respect for women who have to go on bed rest during pregnancy!

Another aspect that made moving more difficult was the drain that was in my head. Any time I wanted to move my body five inches up or down I had to call my nurse. The drain had to remain at a certain level above the drain bag that was catching the extra blood and fluid flowing from my brain. So if I wanted to adjust in bed or even scootch myself up a little higher, I needed to call the nurse. Me being the "don't want to bother them" person that I usually am, I fought the urge to call the nurses yet again to adjust and get more comfortable and instead tried to deal with the pain.

One of my favorite memories from the hospital is Nate reading to me the story in Mark 5, the story of the woman who was healed by faith. She, too, had a hemorrhage, and after touching the hem of Jesus' robe, she was healed! Jesus said to her, "Your faith has healed you. Go in peace" (Mark 5:34).

I tried to have that faith. I knew Jesus could heal me, I knew He could perform miracles, I knew He could make His name great while having His will be done. But some days . . . some days everything just hurt. Some days I just couldn't understand why this would happen to a healthy, young, twenty-six-week-pregnant mom and wife. Some days I just wanted to cry and plead with God the same prayer Jesus cried out before He went to the cross. "Father, if you are willing, take this cup from me; yet not my will, but yours be done" (Luke 22:42).

Life isn't always easy; situations and circumstances we go through can be really hard. Life can just stink sometimes. But here's the thing: God doesn't promise easy, He doesn't promise painless or obvious answers, or even good health all the time. He promises

Himself. That He will *never* leave us or forsake us. That He is working all things out for our good. He promises new mercies every morning. He promises unconditional love. He promises to be our refuge and strength, a very present help in times of trouble. God uses those hard and trying times to grow us and mold us into people that look more like Himself. One of my favorite verses and a story that someone shared with me while in the hospital was from Malachi 3:3. It really fits in with this theme and my struggling with hard days and the "Why me? mentality." It says, "He will sit as a refiner and purifier of silver." This story explained how silver is made and refined. The silversmith needs to place the silver in the fire, in fact, in the very hottest spot of the fire near the middle flames to get rid of all the impurities. While he is refining the silver, he must sit and watch the silver the entire time. He must not take his eyes off the silver because if he leaves it in the fire for even a moment too long, the silver will be destroyed. And how does the silversmith know when the silver is finished? When he can see his own reflection in it.

Friends, this was so encouraging to me. We are going to go through hard times. It's not if, it's when. We need to remember that when we go through the fire, our heavenly Father has His eyes on us the entire time. He will never leave us or forsake us! He knows the exact amount of time that we need to be refined and He will not allow us to remain in the fire for a moment longer than we need. The unbelievably awesome and humbling part of this whole thing is that we hopefully, Lord willing, come out of the fire looking more like our Savior. We can then be a better reflection of Him to those around us who are watching. Life may not always be easy, but it makes it more bearable in those seasons of trial when we remember we are being refined by the master Silversmith Himself.

DAY 6

What gives me the most hope every day is God's grace; knowing that His grace is going to give me the strength for whatever I face, knowing that nothing is a surprise to God.

RICK WARREN

Nate Weeber with <u>Anna Weeber</u>.

September 16, 2016 · Grand Rapids

Friday Morning update: PRAYER WARRIORS, it is time to get back on your knees!

Anna's numbers have elevated (the ones that show spasming) and they are going to be doing an angiogram early this afternoon to take a good look at what is going on. This will tell them if the initial surgery was completely effective and which blood vessels are spasming.

The numbers indicate spasming, but they are very encouraged that Anna isn't showing any physical symptoms, which is a better indicator than the numbers.

Radiation/dye is used with an angiogram.

PLEASE PRAY:

– I want God to work BIG here and blow the doctors' minds! Pray that when they do the angiogram that they will find NO SIGN OF SPASMING. ZIP. ZERO. ZILCH. NADA. Jehovah Rapha, heal my bride!

– Pray that God will protect our baby boy. The radiation used in the angiogram poses decent risks to him. El Shaddai (the One who mightily nourishes, satisfies, protects, and supplies His people), we BEG of you to nourish and protect our little boy! Hold him in your arms and wrap him in a little cocoon of protection!

Father you have had your hand of blessing on this whole process. Thank you for all of the miracles you have already been doing and for protecting my wife and son. In Jesus' holy name I pray that you increase our faith to see Anna and baby through this unharmed! You are the God of Miracles and we watch expectantly!

"I pray that you will begin to understand the incredible greatness of his power for us who believe in him. This is the SAME MIGHTY POWER that raised Christ from the dead and seated him in the place of honor at God's right hand in the heavenly realms. Now he is FAR ABOVE any ruler or authority or power or leader in this world or the world to come." Eph. 1:19-21

The picture below is the FIRST song that came on Pandora this morning when I turned it on in Anna's hospital room.

Pray and EXPECT BIG THINGS!! Love you all! Nate

<u>300 others like this</u> <u>125 Comments</u> <u>136 Shares</u>

Nate Weeber with Anna Weeber.

September 16, 2016 · Grand Rapids

Procedure update: Anna is FINALLY in the operating room! It's been a pretty stressful afternoon.

Please pray for wisdom and guidance for the surgeon's hands and that he will find/take care of what he needs to.

This past hour or two has been so stressful I'm kind of out of words at this point.

Hard to leave Anna in the OR but I know she's in good hands.

Thanks for praying!!

Love you all!

Nate

137 others like this   58 Comments   50 Shares

— ANNA'S STORY —

Hours felt like days as we were waiting to get in the operating room. When you know there is spasming going on and that it may be affecting part of your brain, you want it fixed. Like, yesterday. They told me I would be awake for the procedure because they needed to constantly be asking me questions to see if the spasming was affecting my brain or cognitive abilities. I was actually relieved when I was finally rolled into the operating room. I was just ready to get it over with. The procedure went fairly quickly. About thirty to forty-five minutes. An angiogram is basically an x-ray image of blood vessels after they are filled with a contrast material, or dye. They inserted a catheter into my groin that went all the way up to my brain. This allowed them to check how serious the spasming was and where exactly it was taking place.

Once they found this, they inserted medication through the catheter to help ease the spasming. I remember the doctor telling me I was probably going to feel very warm and taste a silver or copper taste. He did not lie! It wasn't pleasant, but I knew we were close to being done since they were already putting the medication in! The last ten minutes of the procedure were the most painful. Because the catheter they used was so large, when they took it out, the hole by my groin was so large it couldn't just clot on its own so they had to put heavy pressure on it for at least ten minutes.

The man they assigned to put pressure on my leg looked like he was an NFL top draft pick. This man, though fantastic at his job, seemed to not know his own strength. As Ken Davis once joked, "He had muscles in places I didn't even have places!" He was pressing so hard I was about going through the ceiling. I obviously know nothing about medical procedures or routines, so I'm sure he knew he had to use that amount of pressure, but my, was that painful! It was a joy to come out of that operating room and see Nate and my family. God had carried us through one more hurdle.

– NATE'S STORY –

I'll never forget the final moments in Anna's room in the ICU before she was wheeled away for the procedure. I can't remember why, but something was taking longer than it was supposed to. I remember Anna's blood pressure dropping quite a bit from where it had been, which is not good, especially when you want higher blood pressure to keep those blood vessels open to lessen the spasming. As the pressure dropped, I was imagining Anna's blood vessels tightening more and more. On top of that, Anna's vitals were now being monitored on a temporary monitor whose sounds aren't quite as soothing as the normal monitor. And the normal monitor's noises are about as soothing as nails on a chalkboard. The longer we waited, the more this monitor dinged and beeped. It sounded like R2D2 from *Star Wars* was having a meltdown. I was getting so stressed I had to walk out of the room a number of times!

In my Facebook post above, I wrote, "This past hour or two has been so stressful I'm kind of out of words at this point." I was so stressed I'm surprised I got *that* many words out!

Nate Weeber with Anna Weeber.

September 16, 2016 · Grand Rapids

Final procedure update: Woohoo! Procedure went WELL and Anna is awake! Neurosurgeon found some spasming and was able to apply medication to get the blood vessel back open!! Praise the Lord!!

Can't wait to see Anna. OB will be checking on baby soon as well.

Back to monitoring Anna and waiting...

Thank you so much for your prayers!!!

Love you all! Nate

399 others like this   43 Comments   73 Shares

Nate Weeber with Anna Weeber.

September 16, 2016 · Grand Rapids

Friday night update: We are very thankful with how well the angiogram went today!

Only downside is that Anna is in quite a bit of pain and is very uncomfortable - this is getting pretty hard for me to see Anna like this! A little while ago, with tears in her eyes she said, "Nate, I'm just ready to go home." It absolutely breaks my heart to see my bride suffer.

Please pray that Anna will be able to get comfortable and sleep very deeply tonight. Ask our Father to take the pain away and that He will be glorified even in her pain!

Thanks so much for praying! It is still SO encouraging to hear of your faithful intercession. I am so humbled by your faithfulness and persistence.

Baby is still doing well!

Keep praying expectantly for healing!!

Love you all, Nate

230 others like this   54 Comments   67 Shares

— ANNA'S STORY —

The Friday night after the angiogram was *so* painful. My leg hurt quite badly. The doctors needed me to keep my leg as still and straight as possible so the wound wouldn't open up. I was feeling sick. My entire body ached. The anesthesia must have affected me because I ended up vomiting all over my bed. Imagine your body convulsing while throwing up and trying your best not to move your leg, head, or rest of your body. Nurses were trying to hold my leg down. I was trying not to move my head and upper body because of the drain that still needed to be adjusted every time I moved. It was a terrible experience. I don't think I slept more than an hour that night. This is the night that I would rate as the number one worst night at the hospital if we were keeping track.

The hours dragged on, and every time I looked at the clock I got more frustrated. I was willing myself to sleep but I just couldn't get comfortable and I was in so much pain. Lamentations 3:23 says, "His compassions never fail. They are new every morning; great is your faithfulness." I was longing for the morning. A new day, a fresh start. I experienced this verse so tangibly that morning after the angiogram. Nate had gone home to shower and for whatever reason, my mom couldn't sleep so she came up to the hospital bright and early. I was so happy to see her. Sometimes moms just know when their daughters need them. This was one of those times, and I'm so glad God allowed her to not sleep well so she could be there. Just be there. We didn't need to talk, in fact I probably finally slept a while, while she was there, but she was just there.

So often we, myself included, try and find the perfect, most godly words and verses to share with people who are hurting. But I truly feel the most important and the best thing you can do is just be there. In the Bible, when Job had literally lost everything, his friends saw his distress and 1. They wept with him. 2. They literally just sat with Job for seven days and seven nights and no one said a word to him because they saw how great his suffering was.

I think we can all learn from this and personally, it gives me a lot of peace. I don't need to always have the right or perfect thing to say. I don't need to have the perfect verse to share (though at times I believe it is helpful and applicable). More often than not, I believe just being there for people and showing up means more than words can ever say.

DAY 7

Be still, and know that I am God

PSALM 46:10 (ESV)

Nate Weeber with Anna Weeber.

September 17, 2016 · Grand Rapids

Saturday morning update: Praise the Lord for a much better report this morning! Anna doesn't think she got much sleep at all and that it was a pretty long night; BUT, she is feeling much better this morning with less pain in her head. She also just told me she is comfortable which is a huge change from last night!! I can tell she is sleeping right now - she is almost snoring! 😊 Love it. Even her almost-snoring breathing is beautiful. This girl. Man. God blessed me so much in giving Anna to me as my bride!

The nurse told me the "numbers" in her head indicating spasming have gone down which is another huge praise! I'll be getting more info from the doctor at some point to better explain, but for now that's great news. 😊

Anna is still showing NO signs of physical deficiencies/symptoms which is a very good thing. Keep praying that those don't show up.

Yesterday was pretty tough for me, seeing Anna go through everything she did. Had a knot in my stomach all day. It's not always easy to trust but I know that God has a plan and a purpose for everything He is allowing Anna to go through.

Whenever I step back and take a 30,000-foot overview of everything that has happened in the past week, I can so clearly see that our Father had every detail of this planned out from the beginning. Helps me know the future is covered, too. Sometimes I need a little perspective change. 😊

God is good and He is sovereign. Keep praying expectantly!!

"Those who live in the shelter of the Most High will find rest in the shadow of the Almighty.

This I declare about the Lord: He alone is my refuge, my place of safety;

he is my God, and I trust him.

For he will rescue you from every trap

and protect you from deadly disease.

He will cover you with his feathers.

He will shelter you with his wings.

His faithful promises are your armor and protection." Psalm 91:1-4

Love you all!

Nate

353 others like this   40 Comments   83 Shares

Nate Weeber

September 17, 2016 · Grand Rapids

Saturday night update: Thanking our Father for a great day today!

Anna's pain was between a 1 and 4 out of 10 all day. She was also much, much more comfortable than yesterday. That makes for a very happy hubby!

Her spasming numbers were lower this morning which means the spasming blood vessels have opened up a bit. The Doctor explained today that we would like these numbers to keep trending down (blood vessels keep opening), or at least stay the same. Another scan tomorrow morning.

The medical staff has had to increase Anna's blood pressure to make sure blood is pumping well up into her brain. Her heart rate has also increased, which is normal, but they keep asking her if she feels a tightness in her chest or any shortness of breath (this makes a hubby worry).

Anna had an ultrasound of her kidneys today that showed her right kidney is a little enlarged. It could be a sign of irritation, or could just be something with the pregnancy.

Speaking of pregnancy, baby is still doing well. 😊 Good heartbeat and no contractions.

PLEASE PRAY:

– pray that God will allow Anna to sleep very deeply tonight and that she will be able to be comfortable.

– pray that Anna's spasming numbers will continue to decline! Today was Day 7, sort of a peak, but there is still great risk of additional spasming and resulting physical and mental complications. Pray that God will remove that risk and that there will not be the need for another angiogram in this recovery process. Very painful for Anna.

– pray that Anna's heart will keep pumping like a champ and that it won't have any resulting wear and tear from the increased workload it is being forced to take on.

– pray that the enlarged kidney is only due to pregnancy and nothing more.

– please pray that Anna's Arterial Line will continue monitoring her blood pressure well and that it won't have to be replaced again. It's a painful process of removing and placing a line in an artery which has already been done and re-done 3 times.

Anna is busy snoozing away. I bet there aren't too many spouses out there that are thankful to hear near-snoring at night. 😊

I will never forget the sight of Declan laying on his mommy today. This active boy doesn't like to lay down for more than 5 seconds at a time (unless he's sleeping) and he was so content laying his head on mommy's chest for at least a minute or two. Absolutely precious!

Our God is a good, good Father and He loves His daughter, Anna, something fierce! Please pray EXPECTANTLY and in FAITH that He will heal her completely and fully. God loves YOU, He hears YOU, and He is listening!

"He will wipe every tear from their eyes. There will be no more death or mourning or crying or pain, for the old order of things has passed away." Revelation 21:5

As believers, we look forward to the promise of a day without any of this sickness or pain! What a day that will be!

We greatly appreciate your persistent praying!!

Love you all!

Nate

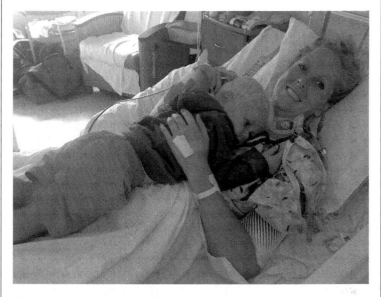

<u>586 others like this</u> <u>92 Comments</u> <u>84 Shares</u>

TO MY SWEET BOY, DECLAN. *You are literally the epitome of the Energizer bunny, you are on the go from sunup to sundown and we absolutely love that about you. Sometimes it gets tiring for mommy and daddy, but we know God created you just the way He wants you . . . He's got huge plans for you, and we wouldn't want you any other way. Today, you, my little pressing-nurse-buttons, running-through-the-hospital-hall, jumping-on-mommy's-bed-boy, were still. Still. You laid by me for the two most precious minutes. This whole thing had to be so hard for you to understand. Why things weren't normal, why mommy was in the hospital, why you had to stay by Papa's and Grandma's houses (which you seemed to love, by the way). You were such a strong and brave boy. Mommy and Daddy are so proud of you. You reminded me of something when you laid your little head on my chest that day. You reminded me that in the hustle and bustle of life, when it seems like everything is going 110 miles per hour, we need to take time to just be still. It's in the stillness we can hear God's voice. It's in the stillness we find rest. It's in the stillness we remember our God, how great He is and all the miracles He's brought us through thus far. You showed me so much love in those two short minutes and I have to imagine that's how God feels when we take the time out of our busy days to be still with Him as well. Thanks, baby boy. I'll love you forever and I'm so entirely thankful God has allowed me to continue being your mommy.*

—Mommy

— NATE'S STORY —

"Whenever I step back and take a 30,000-foot overview of everything that has happened in the past week, I can so clearly see that our Father had every detail of this planned out from the beginning. Helps me know the future is covered, too. Sometimes I need a little perspective change" (from Nate's first Facebook post, Day 7).

About a month before Anna's aneurysm ruptured, we had bought a brand-new chest freezer. It sat in its box in the basement until the Saturday before. Within days of this journey starting, we had three meal trains going, and this freezer was filled to the brim. It was constant little reminders like this that showed us so clearly how God had every detail of this event planned out in advance. By God's grace, He prompted us to buy this freezer just weeks before it would literally be filled to overflowing.

The sovereign God of the universe cares about little stuff like this in your life. I hope you can grasp the significance of that. Matthew 6:26 says, "Look at the birds of the air; they do not sow or reap or store away in barns, and yet your heavenly Father feeds them. Are you not much more valuable than they?" Yes, I am! And so are you! No matter what you are going through today (and I can almost guarantee you're going through *something*), rest in the fact that the King cares about it. The *King*. Who is also your *Papa*. Talk to Him about it.

When I think about all that God has done for us in just these eighteen days, I am overwhelmed with thankfulness. But not only that. I'm also filled with a great sense of *relief*. How comforting is it to know that even on our lowest, darkest day, we're not in this alone? That we don't have to do this on our own?

This is slightly taken out of context, but I think it applies: "When I think of all this, I fall to my knees and pray to the Father" (Ephesians 3:14, NLT).

God had taken care of detail after detail throughout this whole experience. I almost feel guilty that out of everything that Anna endured, it was I who got a front row seat to watch God do His thing. What a show.

DAY 8

Nate Weeber with Anna Weeber.

September 18, 2016 · Ottawa Center

Sunday morning update: God is good, all the time!

Anna's spasming numbers aren't looking quite as good this morning, which indicates that blood vessels are tightening more.

She just had her second Arterial line replaced this morning which hurts this hubby's heart knowing that it's quite painful for Anna.

Please continue praying to the God of miracles that blood will keep getting to where it needs to in her brain and that Anna will have ZERO mental or physical deficiencies/symptoms.

I really, really don't want Anna to have to go through another angiogram and the resulting pain and discomfort, but it may be needed to open the vessels again. I will keep you updated.

Keep praying BIG and BOLDLY to our King reigning on the throne. He is all-powerful and in control! God is good!

Love you all!

Nate

195 others like this   46 Comments   84 Shares

Nate Weeber with Anna Weeber.

September 18, 2016 · Grand Rapids

Sunday afternoon update: Anna's cardiologist has recommended that we only have family visitors at this point. Anna's heart has been "under some stress" from some of the medication and she needs to be kept very relaxed.

Please pray that God will heal Anna's heart and that it will continue to pump strongly!

Anna's head has been hurting pretty bad today, too. Please pray for relief!

Anna will be having another scan fairly shortly to determine if she needs another angiogram today or not.

Please continue to pray in faith for complete healing! Our God is Healer!

Love you all!

Nate

Chris Tomlin - Our God (Live)

M.YOUTUBE.COM

140 others like this   42 Comments   49 Shares

Nate Weeber with Anna Weeber.

September 18, 2016 · Grand Rapids

Sunday evening update: WHEW! Got some good news!

Anna's spasming numbers have come back down so NO angiogram today!

They will scan again tomorrow morning to see what the numbers look like.

Thank you all for praying!!

Please keep praying for:

-STRENGTH and HEALING for Anna's heart that it will not have any negative short or long term effects from the medication

-OPEN blood vessels. We still have quite a few days to go before the risk/concern of Vasospasms goes down.

-Healthy little baby boy. I'm blown away that our little guy hasn't been having any issues yet, but please pray that the occasional radiation they give Anna will not have any negative side-effects.

-COMFORT and PEACE for Anna. She is in pain, uncomfortable and ready to go home! Pray that God will give her peace that passes all understanding.

God is good ALL THE TIME, but it's nice to have some good news after a pretty painful/uncomfortable day for Anna.

"The Lord helps the fallen

and lifts those bent beneath their loads.

The eyes of all look to you in hope;

you give them their food as they need it.

When you open your hand,

you satisfy the hunger and thirst of every living thing.

The Lord is righteous in everything he does;
he is filled with kindness.

The Lord is close to all who call on him,
yes, to all who call on him in truth.

He grants the desires of those who fear him;
he hears their cries for help and rescues them.

The Lord protects all those who love him,
but he destroys the wicked.

I will praise the Lord,
and may everyone on earth bless his holy
name forever and ever." Psalm 145:14-21

Love you all!

Nate

353 others like this 25 Comments 75 Shares

— ANNA'S STORY —

Whew! I feel like these days have just been one roller coaster ride after another! Numbers up, numbers down, good heart news and troubling heart news, blood vessels open, blood vessels closed. God has truly grown my faith so much through this experience. I even find my faith growing as I read back through all of these Facebook posts that Nate wrote. I notice things that I never did before. It's not surprising, I suppose, considering I didn't read half of these posts until months after the aneurysm. My head was very sensitive to light, and looking at a tiny phone with little letters certainly didn't help it feel better. I also found that a lot of activity going on in my room felt very overwhelming to me. As much as I loved seeing Declan every other day or so, his go-go-go personality was often too over-stimulating for my head and/or brain to handle.

As I read back over Nate's post on this day, I notice something interesting in the verses of Psalm 145. Something I've never paid attention to before. It says, "The eyes of all look to you in hope; you give them their food as they need it." (Psalm 145:15). God often only gives us the food, or strength, or provision we need for that day, doesn't He?

I am reminded of the Israelites when they were wandering in the desert. God instructed them to only gather the manna they would need for *that day*. Why would He do this? Isn't it smart to plan ahead, to store up for later? I believe God wants to increase our faith. He says, I'm going to give you just enough for today so that you need to continue trusting Me for tomorrow. He works this way a lot, it seems.

When we need direction in our life, or want to know the outcome of a certain brain aneurysm survivor, He gives us just enough light to take one step at a time, one day at a time. As humans, we want to see the whole picture, the whole path, the final outcome. But God doesn't always work this way. He's using those times to, once again, grow our faith and build our trust in Him. He gives us our daily bread, no more and no less. Praise be to God who blesses us immeasurably more than we ask or imagine while still giving us just enough bread for today.

I can look back and so easily see how God did just that while we were in the hospital. When things seemed to be getting more than we could handle, He'd give us a ray of hope. Often, it was through medical updates, but it was also through people, strangers, family, and friends. It was through our small group laying hands on us and praying in the mighty name of Jesus. It was Nate's entire office taking time out of their work day to encourage us and pray over us. It was a picture on Facebook of a teacher friend who had her entire class praying for us. It was cards, and notes, and goodie bags for the hospital that brought so much joy. It was our front door being decorated with new fall items from dear friends from our church.

God used so many different people and so many different situations to give us hope, faith, and enough light for that day so that we could go into tomorrow knowing God would—once again—provide just enough light to continue pressing on. One foot in front of the other.

DAY 9

How deep the Father's love for us;
How vast beyond all measure.

STUART TOWNEND

Nate Weeber with <u>Anna Weeber</u>.

September 19, 2016 · Grand Rapids

Monday afternoon update: Day 9. God is good. Thankful for the strength and energy He has given Anna to keep going. I can't believe all that she's been through and how well she is doing. I know she is very weary from being poked and prodded so often, not to mention just being in the hospital and now being on bed rest and not being able to get up at all.

PLEASE PRAY:
– Anna's spasm numbers are slightly elevated this morning from where they were at yesterday, but not as much as yesterday and Friday - praise the Lord for that! Please ask that our Healer opens those blood vessels WIDE open!
– I was told this morning that Anna has a slight physical deficiency on her left side. Please ask our Father to restore her strength and bring healing to her whole body!
– Anna is given a medication every 8 hours that is inserted directly into her brain to reduce the Vasospasms. She gets nauseous and vomits every time. She dreads the thought of it and it's pretty taxing on her body. Please pray that it will not make her nauseous and that God will give her extra strength to keep pushing through all this stuff.

Please pray fervently and in faith that our father will HEAL Anna fully.

"The earnest prayer of a righteous person has great power and wonderful results." 1 Peter 5:16b

Friends, this is tough and it is exhausting. But, our Heavenly Father is GOOD and He has a reason for all of this. As hard as it is to believe sometimes, this is part of His sovereign plan!

Pray that Anna and I will continue to trust and have peace amidst this storm. God is good, all the time.

"All glory to him, who alone is God our Savior, through Jesus Christ our Lord. Yes, GLORY, MAJESTY, POWER, and AUTHORITY belong to him in the beginning, now, and forevermore." Jude vs. 25

Love you all! Nate

It Is Well - Kristene DiMarco
& Bethel Music - You Make Me Brave

M.YOUTUBE.COM

<u>231 others like this</u> <u>61 Comments</u> <u>77 Shares</u>

43

Nate Weeber with <u>Anna Weeber</u>.

September 19, 2016 · Grand Rapids

Monday night update: Thanking God for somewhat of a "breather" of a day!

Started this morning out with a phone call that Anna's spasm numbers were slightly elevated, but not to the point of needing an angiogram, thankfully. Also got the news this morning that Anna had a physical deficit on her left side, but was happy to see that it cleared up by the time the doctor came by the next time. Praise the Lord!

Please keep praying that we get a good report on Anna's numbers tomorrow morning and that she continues to show zero signs of a mental or physical deficit!

I'm very, very grateful for an "easier" day for Anna today. She needed it (and so did her hubby)!

Please also pray that Anna will be able to sleep tonight. Because of her physical deficit this morning she is back on the hourly neuro checks straight through the night. Gets old after a while!

We are both still blown away and greatly encouraged by all of your prayer and kind words! Thankful we don't have to go through this alone.

Higher than the mountains that I face

Stronger than the power of the grave

Constant through the trial and the change

Thankful for God's constant, unfailing love!

Love you all!

Nate

Passion - One Thing Remains (Lyrics And Chords/Live) ft. Kristian Stanfill

M.YOUTUBE.COM

<u>265 others like this</u> <u>24 Comments</u> <u>74 Shares</u>

— ANNA'S STORY —

I can't explain it. God had allowed Nate and me to get to a place of such submission to His will. In earthly terms, it doesn't make sense—it wouldn't be humanly possible without the power of Christ working in us. I remember praying to myself some of the words from one of my favorite old hymns, "It Is Well with My Soul."

"When peace like a river attendeth my way, when sorrows like sea billows roll, *Whatever my lot, thou hast taught me to say, It is well, it is well with my soul*" (emphasis added).

I couldn't go on alone. Even though I knew God's will was being done, it didn't make the present any easier. The psalmist says, "My heart and my flesh cry out" (Psalm 84:2). This is where I was. This is the bare, raw, weary me. I knew that the medication was coming every 8 hours and I couldn't do it by myself anymore. I knew that as soon as they put that medication in my drain, within 10 minutes, I would get that sick feeling. The feeling that you have to throw up and it's not a matter of if, it's a matter of when. It was during these times that I had three lifelines. One, I had Christian praise music playing. It was the only thing that could get my mind off of what was happening and onto something greater than myself. Two, I had Nate there beside me every single time. He sat there with me, holding my hand in one of his hands and the barf bin in the other, waiting. The third lifeline was ginger ale. They tried a countless number of nausea medications to help it be more bearable, to take away the sick feeling, but nothing worked. Finally, a sweet nurse who also happened to be a mom gave me some ginger ale to sip while I was feeling nauseated. The nurses were desperate to find anything that might help so she tried a home remedy that helped her kids when they were feeling sick. This was literally liquid gold to me. It helped so much. I was so encouraged. After finding that goodness, the medication didn't affect me as much. It was another small ray of— hope.

— NATE'S STORY —

Imagine the person you love the most in this world—basically the opposite-gendered version of yourself, in my case—being blind-sided by a pain so intense that they're given morphine. And then, less than twenty hours later, they have a hole drilled into the top of their head, a drain inserted, and later that day have a portion of their skull removed, a clamp inserted in their brain and sewn back up. Over the course of the next two and a half weeks, this person will have been poked and prodded to no end—arterial lines (which are painful to begin with) fail and must be reinserted in a different vein almost daily for a week until finally, a more permanent port must be inserted into an artery in their neck. Later, this person will have to have medication inserted into the hole in the top of their head every eight hours for days. And it's going to make them so nauseated that they'll projectile-vomit every time. And they know this. Do you think they would be a pleasant person to be around?

My sweet, sweet Anna. You are truly the most remarkable woman that God has made. The pinnacle of His creation. Your outward beauty is truly second to none, but it pales in comparison to your inward beauty. I'm in awe of your sacrificial love for our family and how you always put others first. I'm in awe of that gorgeous smile of yours that seems to light up any room you walk into, and the friendly, bubbly, happy-go-lucky spirit that goes with it. But how you keep that upbeat, infectious, positive attitude while going through this is beyond me! Part of me wonders if God is having you go through this just so He can show you off a little bit. What a testimony you are of what it looks like to be a woman filled with the Spirit. I can't wait to get out of this sterile hospital room and just go for a walk and hold hands again. You amaze me. I am so blessed to be yours.

I absolutely hated to see Anna in pain. So weak, so vulnerable. As her husband, I felt so helpless. As her protector, it broke my heart to see her hurting, and it was downright awful seeing her lie there after they administered the medication into the hole in her head. Knowing that at any minute the nausea would set in and the vomiting would begin. I would have given anything to take her place!

I wonder if that's how God the Father felt as Jesus was being mercilessly beaten and taking those final steps to the cross. Or even as His Son was being born into a world that would ultimately do this to Him. Amazing that He would allow His only Son to go through something like that for us. Not only to be killed, but in such an excruciatingly painful way.

Truly, how deep the Father's love is for us.

DAY 10

Praise be to the God and Father of our Lord Jesus Christ, the Father of compassion and the God of all comfort, who comforts us in all our troubles, so that we can comfort those in any trouble with the comfort we ourselves received from God.

2 CORINTHIANS 1:3-4

Anna Weeber with Nate Weeber.

September 20, 2016

THIS IS CHURCH, PEOPLE!! I (we) are completely overwhelmed by the outflowing of love and support from our family, friends, and community. You know how to do church, WELL! I don't wish anything like this on anybody and yet hope that at some point in time, every single person will be able to feel this incredible love from the body of Christ. The way you have come alongside us to help with Declan, meals, gas cards, encouraging notes and visits to the hospital has been unbelievable. I keep telling Nate, we are so undeserving of all this! We praise God for His healing and His grace. We praise Him for making Himself known through you, many times. We praise Him for his name being glorified in this whole situation. Thank you for doing life with us, for loving us unconditionally and for your continued prayers! We couldn't have gone through this without our ROCK and REDEEMER and all the beautiful people he has surrounded us with. Thank you so much, from the bottom of our hearts!!

I also want to thank my amazing husband who has fed me applesauce like a baby, made me countless smoothies, stayed by my side everyday and encouraged and prayed with me through it all... While, still keeping all of you up to date. I'm so thankful people get to see a small snapshot of the GREAT man I get to live with and experience everyday!

511 others like this   80 Comments   64 Shares

Nate Weeber with Anna Weeber.

September 20, 2016 · Grand Rapids

Tuesday evening update: Day 10. Hard to believe it's been a week and a half already! God has been good and faithful all 10 days. Even when it has been difficult for me to see.

Started the day out today with news that Anna's spasm numbers were slightly higher, so we weren't too worried about it, but found out about two hours ago that they were the highest they have been yet! Ignorance is "bliss"...

Because her numbers were elevated this morning, they had to give Anna another scan this afternoon. Just found out that her numbers DROPPED! She is down from "severe" spasming to "moderate". Very grateful for that.

47

The doctors are very encouraged that Anna is not showing any mental or physical deficits, even with the severe spasming; in fact, they said they are pretty surprised she isn't having any! Our God is powerful and is taking good care of His daughter!!

Please pray that Anna continues to show ZERO signs of mental or physical deficit and that her spasming numbers continue to decline. Our Heavenly Papa is the Ultimate Healer and I believe that He is going to keep working miracles on Anna's behalf!

Please pray that she can get some sleep again tonight. Still tough to sleep with the hourly neuro checks.

Baby is still doing well!

Thanks for your continued prayers - the same Power that raised Jesus from the dead is at work!

Love you all!

Nate

New Life Worship - Overcome (Lyrics/ Subtitles) (Best Worship Song to Jesus)

M.YOUTUBE.COM

338 others like this   23 Comments   74 Shares

– ANNA'S STORY –

My spasming numbers were the highest they had been. Yet still, no physical or mental deficits. How does that happen? The doctors couldn't believe that even with the severe spasming, I was having no complications. I wanted to shout for joy and say, "*Yup!* That's what my God can do!" He is a miracle worker, He is healer, He is Lord with us, He is the beginning and the end, all-knowing, all-powerful, creator of the universe and creator of me. He is the King of Kings and this was just one more example that shows He was watching out for His undeserving princess.

I remember, multiple times during my stay at the hospital, reciting the Twenty-Third Psalm in my head. It gave me comfort and peace knowing God was directing my path at every turn.

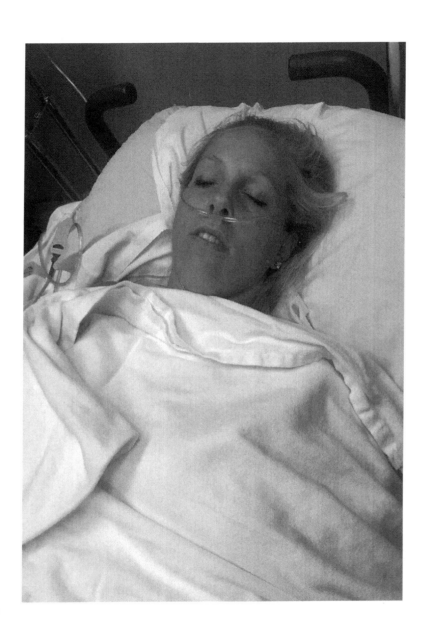

*Nate took this photo at Holland
Hospital thinking this might be the
last picture of Anna alive.*

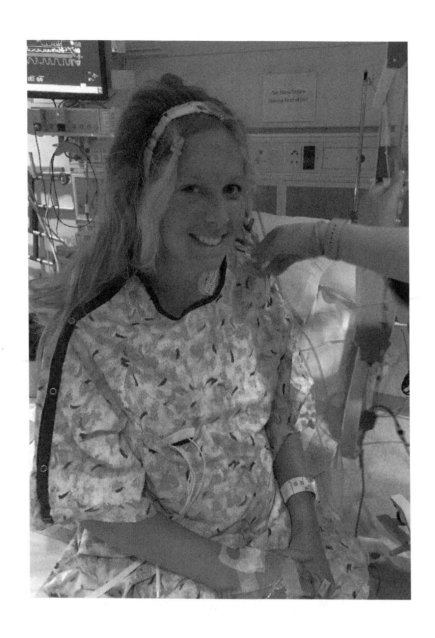

After brain surgery. The bag is filled with fluid and blood that has drained from Anna's brain.

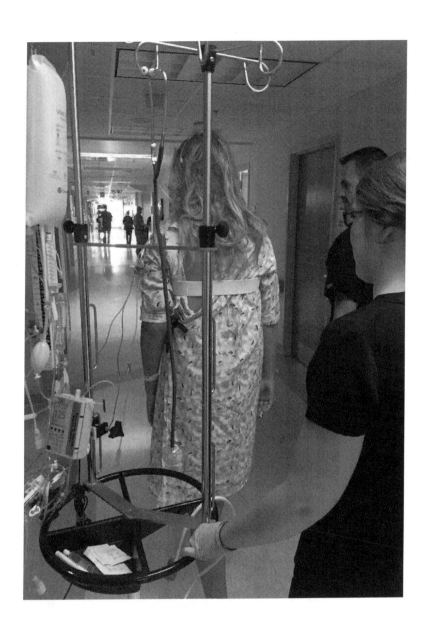

Anna taking her first walk two days
after brain surgery

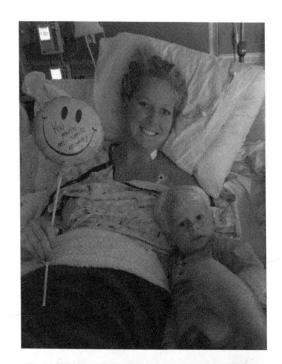

Declan loved to visit mommy at the hospital. Mommy loved it more though.

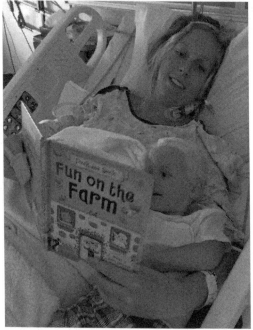

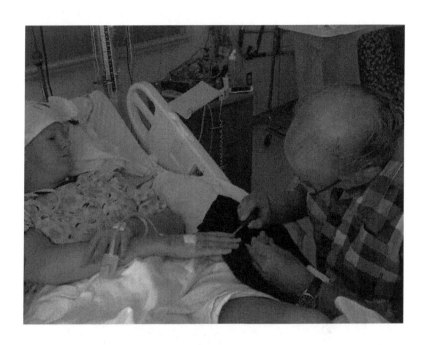

Anna's dad painting her nails.
A busy, hard-working business owner
who still made time to come and visit
us at the hospital every single day.

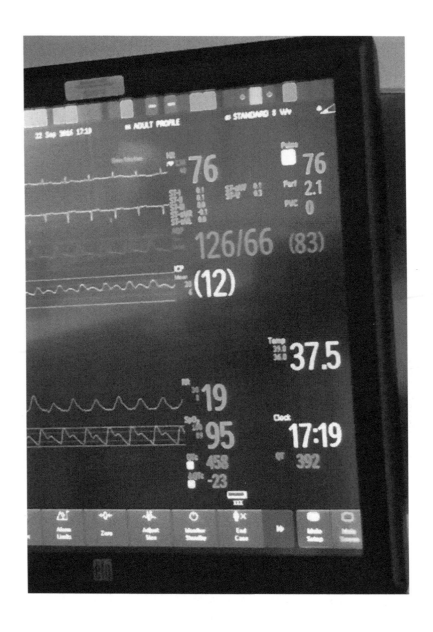

Proof that God still performs miracles
today (see "Nate's Story" in Day 12).

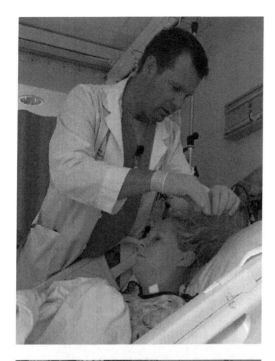

*In the process of
taking the drain out*

*The drain in
Anna's head*

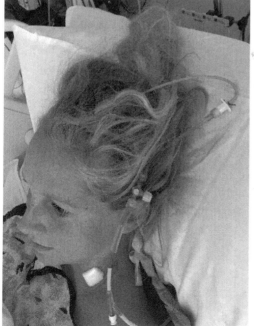

Anna's neurosurgeon,
Dr. Justin Singer

A constant reminder
of God's faithfulness

Nate, Anna, and Declan anticipating the arrival of Hudson

Part of where Anna's hair was shaved for the drain

The birth of our healthy, 10 pound 4 ounce,
beautiful baby boy, Hudson

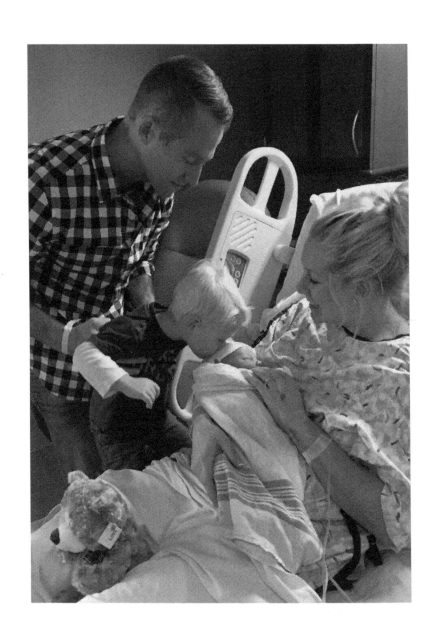

We are all smitten!

The LORD is my shepherd; I shall not want.
He makes me lie down in green pastures.
He leads me beside still waters
He restores my soul.
He leads me in paths of righteousness
for his name's sake.
Even though I walk through the valley
of the shadow of death,
I will fear no evil,
for you are with me;
your rod and your staff,
they comfort me.
You prepare a table before me
in the presence of my enemies;
you anoint my head with oil;
my cup overflows.
Surely goodness and mercy shall follow me
all the days of my life,
and I shall dwell in the house of the LORD
forever. (Psalm 23, ESV)

I didn't so much feel like God was leading me beside green pastures at the moment, but rather I was in a season of "even though I walk through the valley of the shadow of death." Remembering that God in His great power was protecting me with His rod and staff brought me comfort. I remember studying under my Bible teacher in high school, Ray VanderLaan. He would speak often of Psalm 23 and show us pictures of what "green pastures" really looked like in the Middle East. If you're picturing in your head acres upon acres of billowing, knee-high grasses blowing softly in the breeze, guess again. Instead, there are tiny little tufts of grass that sprout up around the edges of rocks where the dew has formed and puddled down the rock to create a miniscule amount of water. Just enough for a little grass to form. When you look at a picture from far away it still looks exactly like a desert, a rocky, dry, barren desert (see https://www.youtube.com/watch?v=kdzhbv2eGxk).

Here's the cool thing. The sheep trust their shepherd. They know that their shepherd will lead them to these "green pastures" where they will get fed. Sometimes the "green pastures" in our lives don't always look billowy and plush and full of life. In fact, sometimes we need to search pretty hard for those little "tufts" of calm, of happiness, of contentedness. But they are there, and our heavenly Father is leading us to them every single day; we just need to have the eyes to look and a heart to trust. Our shepherd knows exactly what we need, and whether we are going through valleys or green pastures, He's going to be there, leading us, guiding us, and paving the way for us.

— NATE'S STORY —

I love how Anna started her Facebook post. "THIS IS THE CHURCH, PEOPLE!!" How true that is. Sure, "a" church can be a nice place where we sometimes dress up, smile, sit neatly in our pews, and pretend that everything is a-okay in life. But this wasn't "a" church, this was *the* church. People from all over the world who were interceding on our behalf. People from all denominations and ethnicities who were coming together and surrounding us with the love of Christ. Phone calls, text and Facebook messages, cups of coffee, cards, gift cards, meals, you name it. Never before had Anna or I experienced the body of Christ to this extent and we were blown away by the compassion and generosity of the church. It was eye-opening to say the least, and was a great reminder of how self-centered we can be when others are hurting. This was the church, and I have never been more proud to be a part of this body God created.

DAY 11

Jesus replied, "You do not realize now what I am doing,
but later you will understand."

JOHN 13:7

Nate Weeber with <u>Anna Weeber</u>.

September 21, 2016 · Grand Rapids

Wednesday afternoon update: GOOD NEWS on Anna's numbers! Just got the report that they are HALF of what they were yesterday morning!! Lower than what they were last night as well.

Jehovah Rapha continues to heal!

Anna said this morning that she slept really well between hourly neuro checks last night, and the nurses said the checks are going great and that she is still showing NO signs of negative mental or physical symptoms!

The doctors have actually started to reduce some of her medication and are discussing possibly being done with the medication that is put directly into her head every 12 hours either tomorrow or Friday! It is very encouraging to hear them talk positively about how Anna is doing and the next steps in recovery.

Depending on what the next couple of days bring, the doctors will start the process of weaning Anna's brain off of the shunt that has been in there for the past 11 days to reduce pressure in her head. They may have to place a permanent shunt in her head that drains directly into her stomach (all under the skin) if her head doesn't properly respond to mitigating the pressure on its own again.

Please pray that Anna's head will get back to doing just what it's done for the past 27 years!

Please also pray for the rest of Anna's body as it continues to heal recover from all of the stress/trauma it has been through and that God will allow for a smooth and quick recovery and transition to "normal life" once this is all over. However; I assure you that our lives will never be "normal" again. Our faith has been deepened to a whole new level and I can't imagine either of us ever taking another moment in life for granted.

Anna has continued to be the same sweet, gracious Anna that we all know through this entire process. I continue to be amazed at the way God has uniquely made her and I am humbled by how she radiates Jesus no matter if she is on her way into brain surgery or being woken up for the hundredth time in the middle of the night only to be poked and prodded once again. So grateful to be her companion.

Just to be clear, I do not mean to ever belittle the staff at the hospital when I say things like "poking and prodding". Anna is receiving the absolute BEST care possible and these doctors and nurses are so gentle and caring! If you ever have an aneurysm, I highly recommend heading to Spectrum in Grand Rapids. 😊

Baby Weebs #2 continues to do well!

Please keep praying. Our God is SO GOOD and SO POWERFUL. And the Creator of the Universe is our Heavenly Papa and loves us as His children. Absolutely mind blowing.

Love you all!

Nate

You Are Good - Israel and New Breed

M.YOUTUBE.COM

342 others like this   45 Comments   83 Shares

— ANNA'S STORY —

There was just so much to be thankful for. Spasming numbers were down, medication is now every twelve hours, weaning off of certain medications, baby is doing amazing, the list goes on. But I couldn't get over the fact of how much my body hurt! Being on bed rest the last number of days had taken a toll on my body that, quite frankly, I didn't know could get any worse. My back, my butt, I needed to just stand up, or even just sit up—like I needed my next breath. Hearing about leaving the ICU soon gave me so much hope. That had to mean more freedom, right? More walking, moving, sitting, anything? As tiring as it was, I couldn't wait to try walking again, I couldn't wait to use these muscles that hadn't been used in weeks.

Friends, family, church members, acquaintances continued pouring in. Visiting, sending cards, gift cards, goodies . . . every single one was so encouraging. We knew we weren't in this alone. We knew this was just one way God was tangibly showing us Himself, through each person, each card, each hug. I kept thinking, *I hope that no one ever has to go through this, something like what I'm going through . . . but at the same time, I hope that every single person gets to experience the body of Christ like we are.*

It is unbelievable; there's nothing like it. We continued to feel so humbled, so grateful for the outpouring of love people showed to us. Even strangers who would write to Nate and myself on Facebook just to say they were praying for us. It baffled us that people would actually take the time, people we didn't even know, to let us know they were praying. I won't ever forget this time in our lives, 1. Because God allowed me to live through a very serious health emergency and 2. Because of the people who blessed us beyond measure and who truly gave us a concrete example of what being the hands and feet of Christ looks like. I will be forever grateful for both.

DAY 12

We will not hide them from their children, but tell to the coming generation
the glorious deeds of the Lord, and his might, and the wonders
that he has done. . . . so that they should set their hope in God and
not forget the works of God, but keep his commandments

PSALM 78:4, 7

Nate Weeber with Anna Weeber.

September 22, 2016 · Grand Rapids

Thursday afternoon update: Day 12. Anna said she slept well last night even with the hourly neuro checks! It's amazing how she can be grateful for a night of terrible, broken up sleep! Proud of my wife's persistent grace through this trial and God's peace.

Anna's spasm numbers were a little higher again this morning, but the trend is going down which is what they like to see. There is also still no sign of mental or physical deficit which is the most important part!

Get ready for some encouragement - we spoke with the neurosurgeon an hour or two ago and he said they are going to be clamping Anna's drain this evening around 6 pm (the shunt that drains excess brain fluid/blood) to make her head start regulating that pressure on its own again. This is the next step in the recovery process. Quite often after an aneurysm a person's head won't regulate again on its own, so a permanent shunt is put in that runs from the brain down to the abdomen. They would like to keep her drain shut until Sunday morning and potentially move her out of the ICU on Sunday if all goes well! Obviously, we don't know if that is going to happen yet, but it is encouraging to hear them talk about forward progress!

The neurosurgeon said if this goes well, she could be out of the hospital a couple days after that (Tuesday or Wednesday)!!

PLEASE PRAY:

– that Our Healer will allow Anna's head to regulate the pressure on its own again. Please pray for comfort for Anna as this process can bring some pretty bad headaches.

– that God will bring COMPLETE healing to Anna's body that we will be able to get out of here next week!

– that little baby will continue to keep developing well. Can't wait to tell him about all of the things God has done!!

"We will tell the next generation the praiseworthy deeds of the Lord, his power, and the wonders he has done...so the next generation would know them, even the children yet to be born, and they in turn would tell their children. Then they would put their trust in God and would not forget his deeds but would keep his commands." Psalm 78:4b&7

Love you all! Nate

437 others like this   51 Comments   105 Shares

– ANNA'S STORY –

I absolutely love Psalm 78. Especially the part where it says, "so the next generation would know them, even the children yet to be born."

Oh, Hudson Steven, this is you. You were the child yet to be born. You are such a miracle. The Lord protected you and mommy from so much. I really believe God just wrapped you in a little cocoon inside of mommy's tummy so you would continue grow-ing into the happy, healthy little boy you are. I remember when you were born. While I was holding you, you would look up at me and when we looked into each other's eyes I would just start to cry. We share such a special bond. It's like we both just knew how much we went through together and how much God protected both of us. To Him be the glory forever and ever!

This is my prayer, that you would recognize the miracle that you are. That you would never forget the praiseworthy deeds of the Lord. We watched miracle after miracle unfold during this process; the wonders He has done have been awe-inspiring. I can't wait to share this all with you someday. Here's the most important part, though. I pray that someday, early on, you would put your trust, put your faith in the Lord Jesus Christ. He is the best thing in life, He is the best thing in death. He created you, He knew you before you were ever born, He handpicked you to do works that He handpicked in advance for you to do. He loves you so, so much and He wants to spend eternity with you.

It is my greatest desire that you would follow Him. Tell the world what He has done, tell the world what He is doing, tell the world about the very best thing, the very best gift ever given. Tell the world about Jesus Christ. I'll love you forever.

—Mommy

– NATE'S STORY –

Speaking of telling wonders to the next generation, here's a story that I will be telling for the rest of my life.

It was at this stage in the recovery process that the doctors shut off Anna's "brain drain" to see if her head would start to regulate the pressure on its own again. If it didn't, the surgeons would have to insert a permanent shunt below Anna's skin to drain excess brain fluid into her abdomen. The ICP (intracranial pressure) monitor took a reading of about every number you can imagine; one of those was a constant reflection of the pressure in Anna's brain.

At any given time, the average person's brain pressure is between a ten and fifteen on the ICP monitor. If you sneeze or cough really hard, it will generally jump up to around a twenty to twenty-five and your head will regulate that pressure back to a normal level. (During the early stages of our journey, Anna's number was as high as a forty.) When the doctors shut off the drain, they look for the numbers to lower on their own.

Our pastor, Clint Echols, had stopped by to pray and hang out for a while. He and I went for a walk in downtown Grand Rapids to check out some of the art exhibits during the ArtPrize art competition. It was a nice break.

As I was making my way back to Anna's room in the ICU, one of the nurses caught me and told me that Anna's number had been elevated for quite some time and the doctors were figuring that she had failed this first test. She told me that they would try again at some point.

Not the news I wanted to hear.

Anna was sleeping, and as I approached her bedside, I looked at the number on the monitor for a while. It floated between a sixteen and an eighteen, but didn't go higher or lower than that. I started praying.

I had learned a lot about prayer over the past twelve days. Since I was a young boy, I was taught that prayer is communicating directly with God, both talking and listening. I was never big on the formality that can often come with prayer. It's a direct conversation with my heavenly Papa. He knows exactly what I'm thinking, so why be formal? But never before had I really "claimed" anything while praying or purposely prayed expectantly or in faith. I learned a lot by both reading Scripture as well as participating in prayer with others who would come to the hospital—others who could school me in both prayer and faith! I wanted Anna to be fully healed, and He knew it. So why not tell Him exactly what I wanted? Why hold back?

I laid out my heart to Jehovah Rapha. I told Him that I wanted Anna to be fully healed, and I claimed her healing in the name of Jesus, the name that is above every other name. Here's where I pulled a Gideon and laid out my fleece for the first time in my life. I told God that I wanted Anna to be fully healed and I said, "If You're going to fully heal her, I want to see the number twelve on that monitor."

It was strange because I fully expected to see the number twelve.

Within thirty seconds to a minute, the number on the monitor worked its way down to a twelve long enough for me to take a picture and then moved back up to the sixteen to eighteen range! It absolutely floored me that the creator of the universe—the sovereign God who holds together the very matter of the universe in His hands—was right there in the room with me and directly responded to my request!

I still, to this day, am trying to wrap my mind around the significance of that number moving. One of two things happened: either (a) God physically changed the number on the screen, or (b) God changed the pressure in Anna's head to reflect the number twelve on the monitor, both of which blow my mind!

Emmanuel. God with us. He's not some distant deity, unconcerned with our ordinary lives. He is right here with us. And He is working *all the time!* It's our job to watch for Him to act, and to be watching *expectantly.*

I don't know why I picked the number twelve; I just picked it out of thin air. As I'm sitting here writing this, I'm just now seeing that it was on the twelfth day of our journey. Knowing that numbers have great significance in the Bible, I did a little digging to see if there is a biblical significance to the number twelve.

One of the biblical meanings of this number is "a completeness or perfection." Wow—isn't that *exactly* what I was asking for?

Just thinking about it gives me the chills.

DAY 13

We are hard pressed on every side, but not crushed; perplexed,
but not in despair; persecuted, but not abandoned; struck down,
but not destroyed. We always carry around in our body the death of Jesus,
so that the life of Jesus may also be revealed in our body.

2 CORINTHIANS 4:8–10

Nate Weeber with Anna Weeber.

September 23, 2016 · Grand Rapids

Friday afternoon update: Day 13. BIG NEWS!!

The doctors clamped Anna's drain last night (shut it off) - she is responding well and her head is back to regulating the pressure on its own!! Praise the Lord! It's a pretty big deal. ☺

Anna's spasm numbers came down again this morning (another praise) so they are done putting the medication in her brain. If everything goes well, they plan to remove the "brain drain" tomorrow or Sunday! Wow. That is good stuff.

Baby still seems to be doing well, also!

A physical therapist should be stopping by today or tomorrow to help Anna begin the process of regaining strength in muscles she hasn't used in two weeks.

She still has a few hurdles to jump before leaving the ICU and leaving the hospital, but God has brought her this far and I believe we'll be back home early next week. If not, it's a part of His plan, and He's been busy at work from the start so we are resting in His timing.

– Please continue to pray in faith for a FULL recovery for Anna and that Baby Weebs #2 will continue to develop unharmed from all that Anna's body has been through. In the limited amount of research I have done, half of the people that have this type of aneurysm don't make it to the hospital alive and those who do have a pretty high chance of having mental or physical deficits. So far, none of these are present! For some reason, our Father is choosing to heal Anna and we are incredibly grateful for that!

"We are pressed on every side by troubles, but we are not crushed and broken. We are perplexed, but we don't give up and quit. We are hunted down, but God never abandons us. We get knocked down, but we get up again and keep going. Through suffering, these bodies of ours constantly share in the death of Jesus so that the life of Jesus may also be seen in our bodies." 2 Corinthians 4:8-10

"And now, all glory to God, who is able to keep you from stumbling, and who will bring you into His glorious presence innocent of sin and with great joy. All glory to Him, who ALONE is God our Savior, through Jesus Christ our Lord. Yes, glory, majesty, power, and authority belong to Him, in the beginning, now, and forevermore." Jude 24-25

I have no doubt in my mind that your prayers have had a direct impact on Anna's recovery. I am forever grateful to you and to God! Keep praying, friends!

Love you all! Nate

Your Love Never Fails - Chris Quilala / Jesus Culture - Jesus Culture Music

M.YOUTUBE.COM

349 others like this 60 Comments 74 Shares

— ANNA'S STORY —

Oh, the excitement of this day! Today was a day for the record books. My drain medication was *done*. My brain drain was shut *off*. My brain was regulating the pressure on its *own*. A physical therapist was coming so I could *walk*. I was feeling like a new woman. God had and was continuing to heal me, completely! What did I do to deserve this?

I stand in awe of my God; I look back at this day and praise Him for more good news. Renewed hope and a ray of light to continue taking one more step. Throughout this experience, God not only reminded me that He's the creator of the universe and the creator of me, He's also a good, good Father. He loves me more than I'll ever be able to comprehend, so much so that He sent His one and only precious Son to die on the cross to take my place.

God's not done with me yet. He still has works that need to be accomplished *by me*. I will live in a whole new light, knowing God could have easily called me Home that mid-September day, but instead, He allowed me to live and grow more like Himself in the process. What an honor that is. What a calling that is, one I do not take lightly. As long as each of us has breath, we all have a calling. We all have unfinished business God wants us to carry out. We were each made with a unique set of gifts and qualities—no one else can complete the task that God wants *you* to complete. I encourage you to finish the race strong—the race that God has prepared in advance for you to do.

DAY 14

The prayer offered in faith will make the sick person well.
The Lord will raise them up. –

JAMES 5:15

Nate Weeber with Anna Weeber.

September 24, 2016 · Grand Rapids

Saturday afternoon update: Day 14. WOOHOO! The doctors are going to remove Anna's drain tomorrow morning and she is going to be leaving the ICU tomorrow as well, Lord willing!

Anna is doing SO WELL!

Lots of praising going on today.

Please pray that Anna's strength will come back quickly. She is a tough cookie, but not using muscles for two weeks straight lends itself to big-time fatigue! We are grateful, though, that Anna is no longer on strict bed rest and is able to stand up once or twice a day and sit in the chair next to her bed.

We don't know what God's plan or purpose is for this, but we know that it is divine and that He has a specific reason for it. I am incredibly grateful that He is allowing Anna's full recovery to be a part of that Plan!!

Sorry for the short post, but I want to get back to watching the Michigan game with my babe. 😊

Praise the King for His healing power!

Love you all (and GO BLUE)!

Nate

804 others like this   70 Comments   114 Shares

— ANNA'S STORY —

More praising today! More of God's overwhelming, undeniable, unbelievable grace! Part of where I see God's grace so significantly in my life is giving me Nate as a husband. He is my very best friend. He's the first person I want to see when I wake up and the last person I want to see (and kiss) when I go to bed. I am so undeserving of a faithful, servant-hearted, loving leader like him. He bought me this sweatshirt (pictured above) to watch the Michigan game with him today. It was such a thoughtful gesture and it finally just felt like a somewhat normal Saturday afternoon—watching football with my man. I can't even begin to tell you everything this man did for me.

When he read in our vows, "In sickness and in health," he was not kidding. He was there for me every single day. He would make and bring up a smoothie for me almost every day. A smoothie with all the best, healthiest ingredients like coconut oil, flax seed, Juice Plus, fruits, spinach, local honey, plant-based protein powder, the list goes on. This sweet man helped nurse me back to health.

I still remember one of the days he brought me a smoothie. I was drinking it and had just received the medication in my drain. The medication that makes me nauseous. And vomit. I should have thought that through better. Within minutes, the entire contents of my smoothie was now on Nate's shirt. Oh, I felt so bad! But of course, he didn't mind a bit. This guy prayed with me, prayed over me, laughed with me, and cried with me. He held my hand, fed me applesauce, refreshed my forehead towel, read me cards and Facebook messages, encouraged me, sang with me, asked questions for me. He was my rock.

I read back through these Facebook posts that he wrote and I so clearly see his love. His obvious love for me, but also his obvious love for Christ. It baffles me how even from the beginning, he was submissive to God's will. The number of times he said, "I don't get it, I don't know why this is happening or how it's going to turn out, but God is still good!" I am blown away and it makes me wonder if I would have the same response if our positions were switched. I always say you can tell a person's character when they are placed in a difficult position. I am so proud of this man. His faith not once wavered. I am honored to call this man my husband and am so thankful God is allowing me to spend more time just being by his side, being his wife. I love you to the moon and back, Nathan C. Weeber!

DAY 15

A cheerful heart is good medicine.

PROVERBS 17:22 (NLT)

− ANNA'S STORY −

Today was a big day—the drain was coming out! It was exciting, nerve-wracking, and exhilarating knowing this was one step closer to going home. *Home*, I absolutely could not wait to get there. When you're away for two weeks, you miss the small things. I couldn't wait for my own bed again, I couldn't wait for my own shower—to finally shave my legs again. I couldn't wait to cook, or even use my own toilet without a nurse in the room!

Back to reality—so many thoughts were running through my head, the main one being, would my brain still be able to regulate the pressure and drain the blood on its own again? "Don't be afraid, for I am with you. Don't be discouraged, for I am your God. I will strengthen you and help you. I will hold you up with my victorious right hand" (Isaiah 41:10, NLT). The number of times God's truth rang through my head while I was in the hospital was supernatural. I know it was only from God. This was just one more way God increased my faith through this process. He never let me forget His promises or His Word. The doctor came in to remove the drain, and I sat there so still, wondering if I would feel anything. So many thoughts were going through my head. I was trying to imagine what it was going to feel like or if I would get sick or nauseated.

All of a sudden I hear the doctor say, "Okay! Here it is!" I look at him and say, "You're done already? It's out?" I hadn't felt a thing. Thank You, Father! I couldn't believe how long the drain actually was—about five inches in length. We of course had to get a picture of it with the doctor because, well, why wouldn't you? The drain came out and as always, Nate was by my side.

I knew our families were coming up later that day and an idea started forming in my mind. An idea that some would call mean and terrible considering all we had gone through, but an idea that would perhaps just show that the Anna with the sense of humor was still in there. Now, my uncle Larry Genzink is the head of Radiology at Spectrum Health and he would visit quite frequently after he was

65

done with work for the day. Something my parents knew and something I was so grateful for. I felt so proud having all the doctors and nurses know that this smart guy, the *head* of radiology, was my uncle.

A couple hours after the drain came out, my dad called Nate to let him know he was on his way up to see us. This was my opportunity. My parents knew the drain was coming out and I knew they were obviously hoping I wouldn't have any negative side effects or cognitive impairments from it. I finalized the details in my mind and waited for my dad's arrival.

When he walked into my hospital room, my face lit up and in a happy, cheerful voice I said, "Hi, Uncle Larry!" The look on my dad's face is something I will never forget! It was a look of total dismay and disappointment. Then I looked at Nate's face. He had no idea I was planning this, so his face was just as stunned as my dad's! His reaction only confirmed to my dad that something was terribly wrong.

Walking toward me, my dad then said, "Yeah? Do I look like your Uncle Larry?" The poor guy thought that his own daughter didn't recognize him. That was enough, I couldn't take it any longer. I burst out laughing and told them it was all a joke. Thankfully, after it all sank in, they started laughing too and it was the story to be told for the next few days. Sometimes, a little laughter is just the perfect medicine.

— NATE'S STORY —

Not cool, Anna, not cool. Anna is finally to the point of recovery where her drain has been taken out, she's about to leave the ICU, and she doesn't recognize her own father. I can't tell you how my heart sank when my father-in-law, Steve, walked in and Anna "mistook" him for his brother, Larry. In my mind, I'm assuming that now that the brain drain has been removed, the pressure was building again to the point where Anna was losing cognitive ability. My heart immediately sank, and it sank low. And the look on Steve's face showed that his heart did the same! Thankfully, this was just a nasty prank and a good sign that Anna's humor was still intact! The three of us will never, ever, forget that moment.

But seriously—not cool, Anna, not cool.

Lord my God, I called to you for help,
and you healed me.

PSALM 30:2

Nate Weeber with <u>Anna Weeber</u>.

September 26, 2016 · Grand Rapids

Monday morning update: GOD IS ON THE MOVE (and so is Anna - OUT of the ICU as of yesterday 😊 !!

Anna had her shunt (brain drain) removed yesterday as well and is doing great!

I am absolutely floored by the healing power of our God.

Bless God for His goodness!!

Love you all!

Nate

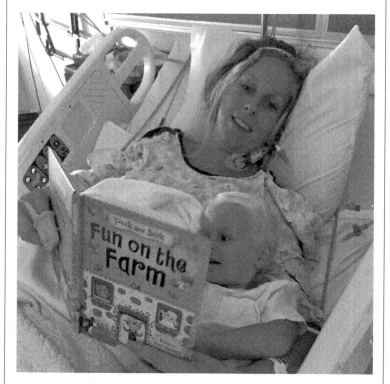

<u>825 others like this</u>   <u>120 Comments</u>   <u>107 Shares</u>

— ANNA'S STORY —

"I will exalt you, Lord, for you lifted me out of the depths . . . Lord, my God, I called to you for help, and you healed me" (Psalm 30:1-2). One step closer to *home*! This new "normal floor" room was fantastic. Less beeping, less nurse checks, less pills, more walking. We'd been praying for this day for what seemed like forever. It was finally here and it was good. God is good. Declan came up to the room today again and I read to him one of his favorite books. *Fun on the Farm*. This boy loves all things farm, animals, tractors, and scoops. It was such a treat to take my mind off of being "patient" and just get to be mommy again, even if only for a few moments. How I missed home with my boys. Soon enough it would be here. Soon enough, Lord willing.

— NATE'S STORY —

What a relief it was to be out of the ICU! Just knowing that we were in the *Intensive* Care Unit added a significant amount of weight to the situation. Until Anna's aneurysm, I had never even been to the ICU in a hospital before, let alone spent two and a half weeks in one. In my mind, this was where the "worst of the worst" medical cases go (which is true). I was so glad Anna could finally move to a floor and a room that was quieter. We received the absolute highest level of care while we were in the ICU, but it was nice to be done with the constant beeping, footsteps, and commotion. The nurses only had to check Anna's vitals and cognitive abilities every four to eight hours, so she was finally able to get some rest.

But it was still a hospital. At this point, we were chomping at the bit to get *home*. To just lie on our own bed together at home and stare at the ceiling. *Our* bed. *Together*. I knew our lives would never be the same. I knew that this journey would turn the everyday-mundane into extraordinary. I would later find out that this was an understatement!

DAY 17

If you, then, though you are evil,
know how to give good gifts to your children,
how much more will your Father in heaven give good
gifts to those who ask him.

MATTHEW 7:11

– NATE'S STORY –

I'm so thankful to have grown up with a correct understanding of who Yahweh is. It's true that He is the all-powerful, ultimate ruler of the universe, but He's also my heavenly Papa—my Daddy. Such a paradox.

Matthew 7:7-11 talks about what effective prayer looks like, and to me, describes it in two parts.

The first is *persistence.* Verses seven and eight say, "Ask and it will be given to you; seek and you will find; knock and the door will be opened to you. For everyone who asks receives; the one who seeks finds; and to the one who knocks, the door will be opened." There's not too much I can add to this—its meaning is pretty self-explanatory. If you feel like you're not getting an answer right away, keep asking.

The second is *perspective.* Verses nine through eleven say, "Which of you, if your son asks for bread, will give him a stone? Or if he asks for a fish, will give him a snake? If you, then, though you are evil, know how to give good gifts to your children, how much more will your Father in heaven give good gifts to those who ask him!"

I've always appreciated viewing my relationship with God as that of a father and a son. One of the reasons is that I have an incredible earthly dad who is a very godly man. Someone I deeply respect and admire as a strong man of character and resolve (he's a man's man), but he's also got a very tender, giving heart. My dad is pretty much Iron Man (in my view), but he's also a giant teddy bear. He's given me a great earthly picture of what my heavenly Father is like.

Now, as a dad, this passage resonates with me on a much deeper level. Whenever I read it, I picture my son, Declan, asking for his typical morning snack—Cheerios and cranberries. Why on earth would I give him a stone? Or a snake? Or anything that wasn't related to satisfying his hunger? I wouldn't. It's the same with God—only *intensified*. He loves you with a deeper, more intense love than any earthly love you will ever experience. How comforting.

My first or second time stopping home while Anna was in the hospital, I received a timely piece of mail that contained, among other things, a small card with Isaiah 41:10 on it as well as a picture of an adult hand with a tiny infant's hand grasping tightly at one of the adult's fingers. I say it was a timely piece of mail because that's precisely how I felt; like I was an infant just hanging onto my Daddy's finger for dear life.

Isaiah 41:10 says, "So do not fear, for I am with you; do not be dismayed, for I am your God. I will strengthen you and help you; I will uphold you with my righteous right hand."

Our heavenly Papa loves giving good gifts to us and is right by our side when we're going through the valley. Trust and *rest* in those promises.

DAY 18

I have heard your prayer and seen your tears;
I will heal you.

2 KINGS 20:5

Anna Weeber

September 28, 2016

God is so good and so faithful! He is a powerful God of miracles and second chances- all of which I've experienced these past two and a half weeks! As I prepare for my HOME-going TODAY, I feel so excited and blessed and yet I can't help but feel somewhat guilty, because as I celebrate healing and going home, there is another family from our HCHS community, Mr. Kevin Witte who is a teacher, coach, husband, and father to three little kids that went HOME to be with Our Heavenly Father last night after a terrible accident. My heart breaks for this family and I can't help but wonder, why me? Lifting this family and the HC community in my prayers.

I want to thank, from the bottom of my heart, all the people who have supported, prayed for, shared posts and sent gifts and cards on my behalf. We are so humbled and so grateful for this community of believers. I want to share just a few of the sweet gestures as it may encourage you or give ideas to do for someone else who's been in a situation like mine. It would be impossible to share EVERYthing EVERYONE did for us- please just know we appreciate you all so, so much and praise God HIS name can be made known even during hard times. We have our church family and friends making freezer meals, people mailing cards to our home and the hospital, some including gift cards or gas cards, anonymous gifts dropped off at the hospital for myself and Dec to play with when he visits me at the hospital. Snacks and goodie bags, countless people dropping by to say hi and praying for healing in the mighty name of Jesus. Our wonderful parents watching Dec and taking care of him this entire time, brother Mark taking time off work and coming home from CO after he heard the news. Some sweet friends from church giving me a warm blanket as hospitals can get quite chilly, other friends decorating our front door at home with beautiful fall decor. My dad painting my nails in the ICU and mom giving me a pedicure. Nate's entire office coming to visit and praying healing over us, people coming to take Nate out for lunch or just looking around at Art Prize entries for a little break. Neighbors mowing our lawn and watering flowers, pumpkin Blizzards being brought up and apple crisp being made. People sending Facebook messages of hope and encouragement... People we don't even know. Friends from high school I haven't talked to in years sending cards and "cheering" me on. 2nd grade teachers having their entire class pray for me, the list goes on.

THANK YOU to each one of you! I pray someday I will have the opportunity to bless you all as much as you have blessed me and my family in these last weeks.

Love you all so much!

Anna

283 others like this   246 comments   117 shares

Nate Weeber with <u>Anna Weeber</u>.

September 28, 2016 · Ottawa Center

HOMEWARD BOUND with my bride!! Praising our Father for all He's brought us through!!!

<u>1.5k others like this</u> <u>192 Comments</u> <u>97 Shares</u>

— ANNA'S STORY —

Home! This was it! God had just brought us through the journey of a lifetime and I was walking away, heading *home* without one single complication. I had defeated the odds. Doctors were elated. Prayer warriors, praising! What a journey it was. Even just climbing into our car felt so surreal, felt so good again. Riding home with Nate's hand in mine, life couldn't get any better. I was here, I was with him, God had showed up and we had a front row seat. I was perfectly, completely, unbelievably healed.

As happy as this day was for me, for us, our hearts were sad-dened by the news that a local Holland Christian teacher had lost his life in a very serious accident. Both growing up in the Holland Christian school system, Nate and my hearts were heavy from this loss. This man of God had a wife and three beautiful children he left behind. I couldn't help but think, *Why would God save me and allow this father of three, this influential coach and teacher to die?* I couldn't help but feel guilty. To bring it one step further, how come God answered our prayers when there are millions of others who pray just as often and just as hard for a loved one, yet don't get the healing outcome they ask God for?

I don't think we'll ever know this side of heaven but we cling to the promise that we serve an all-knowing, all-powerful God who doesn't make mistakes. I learned that we shouldn't be asking the question, "Why, God?" But instead, "How is God going to use this?" We cling to the promise that those who have gone before us are in the presence of Christ our Savior. Praise be to God! To the one who gives and takes away.

— NATE'S STORY —

It was so wonderful just to be able to open the car door for Anna again. This woman is the epitome of "magnificent" in every sense of the word. Just thinking about how truly incredible she is almost brings tears to my eyes. She is far, far out of my league and this is something I remind her of on a regular basis. Being able to once again treat her like my queen in this small way made me giddy.

How surreal to be showing my bride the parking ramp where I parked every day; the restaurants I would walk to; the route I drove over forty times in the past two and a half weeks—while crying out to God for her healing. But this time, with my fully healed wife. My *direct* answer to prayer.

"Praise be to the God and Father of our Lord Jesus Christ!" (1 Peter 1:3).

GOD'S GRACE NEVER ENDS: WHERE WE ARE NOW

Let all that I am praise the Lord;
may I never forget the good things He has done for me.

PSALM 103:2

Anna Weeber with 2 new photos.

September 30, 2016

I gave in and got that trendy new half shaved head haircut.... NAILED IT! 😄
#thankyoubrainsurgery #mostexpensivehaircutever #Godisgoodallthetime

305 others like this   40 comments   3 shares

— ANNA'S STORY —

When God refines you through the fire, He brings you out better than you were before. Looking back at all of this, now eight months ago, we can truly say we are better than we were before all of this happened. We live each day a little more fully. We live in the present, knowing only God holds our tomorrows. Our faith has been deepened; we were privileged to see God work so tangibly on our behalf often right in front of our eyes. We have a whole new appreciation for the body of Christ. We had front row seats in witnessing the power of prayer. Our marriage has never been stronger—a new appreciation for your spouse develops when you go through a valley like this. By the grace of God we got through this. By the grace of God I was healed.

From a medical standpoint, I am better off now than I was before the ruptured aneurysm. The first obvious reason is I no longer have a ticking time bomb in my head. I will have CT scans every three to five years from here on out to make sure no other aneurysms form. This precautionary scan will give me such peace of mind, considering I have a slightly higher chance of getting another aneurysm because I was so young when this happened. The second reason is that I no longer have headaches. Before the aneurysm, I would have two to four headaches a week since high school. My neurosurgeon said the aneurysm was most likely causing those headaches. Unbelievable. So not only did God choose to completely heal me, He decided to take it one step further and make me better off than I was before. Only grace. Only God.

Every trial God allows us to go through is a platform He uses to reveal Himself both to us and through us. We saw His grace, His goodness, His healing, His power. A verse I came upon recently was John 11:4. It says, "This sickness will not end in death. No, it is for God's glory so that God's Son may be glorified through it." I truly believe God allowed me to live so that we could make His name *great*! To God be the Glory! It is our prayer that our story has reminded and inspired others as well. God chose to use our platform for others to see how *great* He is. For whatever reason, our story started getting lots of media attention. The following is my journal entry from January 30, 2017, that summarizes a bit of how I was feeling.

"We continue to feel so humbled at how God is using our story. God, I pray You would rid myself of any pride that may creep in. The focus is *You*, Father. Help me to remember that always. You have opened up doors in local newspapers, TV news stations, Spectrum Health Newsletters, and we gave You glory. Now, You've opened up more doors. *People* magazine, *Woman's World, The 700 Club.* It's unbelievable how You have used our story to spread Your fame. We feel humbled and honored. Father, may we point all of this back to

Nate Weeber with Anna Weeber.

October 8, 2016 · Ottawa Center

HOME Update: Some of you have been asking for a post-hospital update, so here it is!

Anna continues to recover very well. She still gets tired fairly quickly and has a constant mild headache (both of which are normal and expected due to almost-zero physical activity for 3 weeks and the blood still working its way out of Anna's brain), but other than that she is doing phenomenally well!

Declan loves having his mommy and daddy back home (especially his mommy), and mommy and daddy love being back with their little buddy! We are so grateful that our parents were able to step in the gap while we were in the hospital.

Baby Weebs #2 seems to be doing well, too!

We are so thankful for all of you! We continue to be inundated with cards, frozen meals, hot meals, lukewarm meals (huh?), gift cards, encouragement, you name it. This has changed our perspective on what it means to care for others! You have truly been the hands and feet of Jesus and we are so humbly grateful to be on the receiving end.

It is SO GOOD to have my babe back home. Oh. My. Goodness. This woman is incredible and I am so grateful to our Heavenly Papa that He saw fit to restore her 100%.

My apologies in not getting an update out sooner, but it has been wonderful adjusting to normal life and putting this on the back burner for a bit.

We went apple picking at Crane's today - turns out Summer was replaced by Fall while we were in the hospital! 😄 🍁 🍎 🍂

Love you all!

Nate

1.1K others like this   85 comments   69 shares

You. Continue opening up doors if it is Your will. May we be a light in this dark world. May we share hope for the hopeless and healing for the broken. I feel You urging me, saying, "You have a story to tell—people are responding! I gave You a platform, now use it for My glory!" Father, bless our story, bless this book. May people see You and come to know You through it. Spread Your fame like wildfire!"

To my love,

You don't know. You don't know the impact you had on me during this trial. Your faith. Your unconditional love. Your encouragement. Your constant presence. Your prayers. You showed me love in a way I've never experienced before. You were there. You stayed. You didn't give up on me when things got tough. You stood by your word to stay, in sickness and in health. You helped carry me through a time when I couldn't do it on my own.

You don't know. You don't know the number of lives you touched just by writing those posts. Your expectant faith. Your big and bold prayers. Your obvious love for me by calling me your "bride." Hearts were softened, people were encouraged, and lives were changed.

You don't know. You don't know what a shining example of Jesus you were to me and so many others. Your servant heart. Your humble nature. Your sweet, encouraging demeanor. You were a shining example of what it looks like to praise Him in the storm.

You will never know how proud I am of you. Of how you handled one of the most frightening, difficult, trying times in our lives. How you trusted Jesus Christ with every inch of your being. How you didn't know the outcome but still wanted to give God the glory.

You have never stopped tryin' with me, Nathan Weeber. Never stopped opening my doors or holding my hand. You never stopped dating me or telling me I'm beautiful. You never stopped showing me a kind of love I've only dreamed of. I am so undeserving of you and I will spend the rest of my days reminding you of this. You are my very best friend and forever love. I'm so thankful God has chosen to heal me and give us more time together. I love you more than words can say.

Your Anna